THE
ISLAND OF BUTE

by IAN S. MUNRO

DAVID & CHARLES

NEWTON ABBOT

To Mary
and
all her kin

ISBN 0 7153 6081 7

*Set in eleven on thirteen point Baskerville
and printed in Great Britain
by Latimer Trend & Company Ltd Plymouth
for David & Charles (Holdings) Limited
South Devon House   Newton Abbot   Devon*

CONTENTS

ILLUSTRATIONS

ILLUSTRATIONS

8

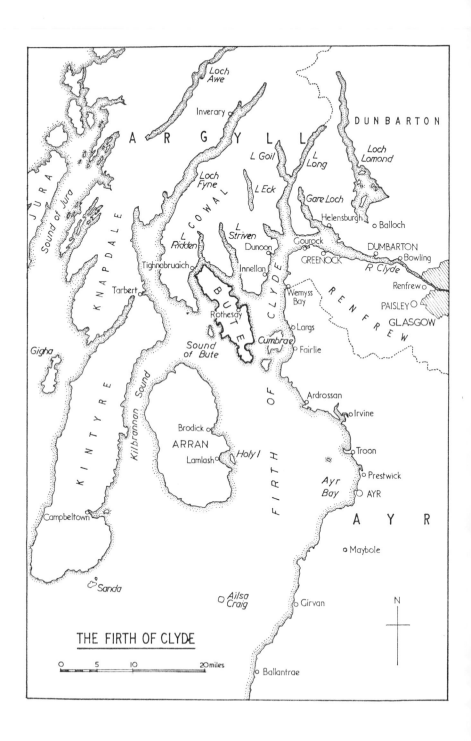

THE FIRTH OF CLYDE

1   INTRODUCTION TO THE ISLAND

THE landlocked waters of the Firth of Clyde encompass such a variety of long peninsulas, deep-cut bays, fiord-like sea lochs, and narrow kyles, that it becomes difficult to distinguish island from mainland. This is particularly so with the Island of Bute, where the coastline is seldom more than a few miles from neighbouring land; at its northern end the distance shrinks to a matter of yards across the beautiful Kyles of Bute, which separate the island from Argyll.

Another factor which diminishes insularity is the proximity of heavily populated Glasgow and its environs, whose citizens have adopted the town of Rothesay as a holiday centre, sometimes even without realising its geographical position on an island. Yet the remarkable thing is that Bute has maintained its individual character, and over the centuries has played a distinctive and sometimes unique part in most aspects of human life and development.

Its position near the centre of the early sea-routes, and the attractions of sheltered harbours, gentle slopes, and fertile land, ensured a continuous sequence of visitors, welcome and unwelcome, from Neolithic times onward. Bronze and Iron Age men, Celtic saints and missionaries, Viking raiders, champions of Scottish Independence, attackers and keepers of the Castle, kings from both sides of the border, all left their mark on the island, and it can be said that every phase of Scottish history is reflected in the stones and monuments of Bute.

Geographically Bute is one of seven islands (three with centres of population) comprising the county of Bute, which shares with Orkney and Zetland the position of being the only Scottish counties that are wholly insular. Arran is the largest of the seven, but Bute is the main island, the administrative capital, and the chief population centre.

Situated on the Firth of Clyde, Bute lies south of Argyll, with Ayrshire to the east, Renfrewshire to the north-east, and the island of Arran and the Mull of Kintyre to the south-west. It is 5 miles west of the nearest point on the Renfrewshire and Ayrshire coast, 7 miles from a port, but only a few hundred yards by ferry across the narrows of the Kyles of Bute to Argyll.

Bute is 15½ miles long, varies from 1¼ to 5¼ miles in breadth, and has an area of 31,000 acres. One-third of the land is arable, and of the remainder the greater part is under heather. Although there are extensive stretches of wild steep moorland, the highest hill is just over 900ft. Loch Fad, which is over 2 miles in length and ¼ mile in breadth, is the largest of several freshwater lochs, the other inland waters being Loch Ascog, with an area of approximately 70 acres, Loch Quien 50 acres, Loch Greenan 12 acres, and the Dhu and Bull Lochs each less than 10 acres.

The island has three natural divisions: the northern part, which lies close to Argyll and is mainly wild moorland, bog, and hilly ground rising up to nearly 1,000ft; the middle part around the valley and lochs that almost cut the island in two, and where the wide sweep of Rothesay Bay provides a harbour and setting for the main town; and the southern part of plateau and steep escarpment bounding the wide plain between Kilchattan and Stravannan.

To the west, approximately a mile from St Ninian's Bay, lies the adjacent island of Inchmarnock. Although only 2 miles in length, with 5 miles of coastline, it has had a significant part in the story of Bute, particularly in archaeology and early history, and its two farms at either end of the 600 acre island are still worked by residents, who ferry supplies across the firth from the shore at St Ninian's Bay.

The geological structure of Bute has many interesting features,

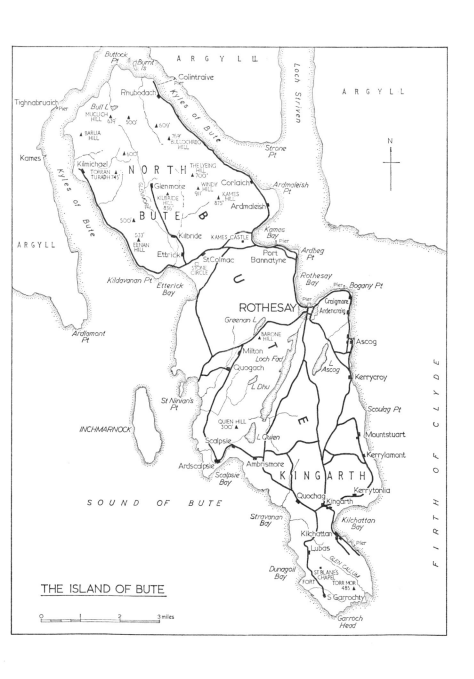

THE ISLAND OF BUTE

0   1   2   3 miles

the most striking being the contrast between the northern and southern parts of the island. This arises mainly on account of the Great Highland Fault, which starts near Stonehaven on the north-east coast, proceeds south-west across Scotland, finally reaching Bute and cutting across its central plain by way of Rothesay Bay, Loch Fad, Loch Quien, and Scalpsie Bay.

In this valley the crack can be clearly seen to divide the rocks and soils of the two regions—to the north the igneous rocks, the metamorphic schists; to the south the sedimentary, the slates, the old red sandstone, and some calciferous sandstone lavas to intrigue geologists.

The geological pattern and structure of the island is, of course, responsible for much of the scenic beauty and natural attractions. Within a comparatively small area there is a remarkable variety of scenery, ranging from hard rocks and heather-covered hills around the Kyles of Bute, by way of numerous sheltered lochs and richly coloured sandy bays to the steep escarpments beyond Kilchattan, and the cliffs and rocky points around Garroch Head. The contrast between the smooth rounded hills of the old red sandstone and the sharper schists is striking.

The climate of the island is equable—the monthly mean temperature over a very long period has never been higher than 66° F in summer, and only once below 38° F in winter. The rainfall is reasonably light for the area, with a yearly average of 55·6in. There is very little snow and no fog. Evidence of mild winters and absence of severe frosts can be seen in the growth of numerous palm trees, fuschia bushes, etc. In a district of notoriously uncertain and changeable weather, amounts of sunshine can vary greatly from month to month and year to year. Yet monthly totals in excess of 200hr are usually recorded in at least one of the summer months, May and June offering the best prospects.

The varied nature of the landscape, together with the temperate climate, makes for great richness and variety of flora and bird life. The birds in particular are unusually abundant, with a recorded list of well over 100 residents and regular visitors.

In some respects, though surprisingly not all, Bute is dominated by Rothesay, the main population centre, the administrative county capital, and the chief holiday resort. In 1907 Neil Munro, a famous chronicler of the Firth of Clyde, described Rothesay's position as 'snugly tucked in a bay that must have given much joy to its discoverers as it has to millions since'. Now the only port on the island, Rothesay's sheltered bay continues to provide safe anchorage and a spacious harbour, with the modern addition of new pier terminal buildings to welcome the continuing millions.

The pier is indeed a focal point, providing first and last impressions for those many visitors, and arousing a variety of emotions in exiles leaving or returning to their native island. The stranger stepping from a steamer gangway to Rothesay pier is greeted by a familiar railway-station type loudspeaker announcement, followed by a selection of more or less appropriate Scottish music. But if he turns his eye from shore to sea, he is introduced to one of the most glorious views imaginable. Across the gentle curve of the bay, where the little yachts lie at anchor, stand the shapely purple-coloured hills beyond Loch Ridden and Loch Striven, while round the point the silvery waters of the Firth lap the green shores of the island along the narrow Kyles of Bute. On the other side, behind those very ordinary streets of Rothesay, the sentinel peaks of Arran's Sleeping Warrior form an extraordinary backcloth to the town.

Such contrasts are typical of Bute. Drabness rubs shoulders with uncommon beauty, the past mingles with the present, and that strange Scottish dichotomy between Highland and Lowland, spiritual as well as geographical, finds ultimate expression in an island that has a heart deep in the Highlands, yet at times almost belongs to those Lowland visitors.

The pier itself is something of a meeting place for those

15

contrasts, a frontier post between visitor and resident, between colour and drabness, between Highland and Lowland (in actual physical fact it stands almost on the Highland Fault line) —and, above all, between present and past. It remains something of a symbol of the bustle and excitement of the great days of huge fishing fleets in the adjoining double harbour, and for some the even greater days when hour after hour, from early morning until evening, a succession of little steamers with paddles churning and gaily coloured funnels smoking, arrived or departed with crowded decks of passengers.

Their names are almost a litany, and should be inscribed as a memorial somewhere on Rothesay pier, as they are on the models and photographs in local taverns, and in the memories of older Clydesiders—the *Columba,* the *Atalanta,* the *Davaar,* and the *Galatea; Glen Sannox* and *Glen Rosa, Marmion,* and *Lord of the Isles; Kylemore* and *Mercury, Lucy Ashton* and *Iona;* the *Caledonia* and the *Waverley.* The list seems endless.

Yet it is fact and not legend which records that these little ships made over 100 daily calls at Rothesay in the summer of 1913, and on occasions three would berth simultaneously at the main pier, with one at either end, and another waiting in the bay. Little wonder that the familiar setting can communicate something of the excitement of the past, and retain at least a sense of the magic that remains.

Despite population fluctuations which, as will be seen later, have been quite spectacular, Rothesay has statistics as well as natural and acquired assets to justify its monopoly of most aspects of the economic, commercial, welfare, and community life of the island.

As a holiday centre it has many advantages of setting, outlook, accommodation, and communication facilities, but in an island of this size it may be argued that excessive concentration in one corner has serious drawbacks. In this, as in several other respects, the role of Rothesay might be seen as centralising and co-ordinating rather than monopolising. The island still

Page 17 (*above*) The Firth of Clyde: as seen from Rothesay's Municipal Golf Course on the slopes of Canada Hill; (*below*) inland scene: the farm of Lochly has a sheltered setting beside the quiet waters of Loch Fad

Page 18 (top) Rothesay Bay: a summer Sunday in 1894 during regatta weekend. Apart from the yachts, well-known steamers including *Glen Rosa*, *Jeanie Deans*, *Viceroy*, and *Marchioness of Breadalbane* can be recognised; (centre) regatta day: in the early eighteen-nineties, highlighting the two funnelled *Galatea* and *Marchioness of Breadalbane*, with yachts in the background; (foot) the harbour in Victorian times: the houses remain practically unaltered, although transport has changed radically

retains a life of its own—perhaps the unusual but surprisingly healthy agricultural pattern is a factor here—which is more than parochial or narrowly social. And for the thousands of visitors who have grown to love it, Bute is much more than Rothesay—it is an island of surprising peace, great beauty, and infinite variety.

2   THE ENVIRONMENT

THE rocks of Bute hold great interest for the geologist seeking evidence concerning the origins of the island. Although it cannot claim the spectacular geological fame of neighbouring Arran, Bute shares several of the larger island's characteristics, sometimes on a small scale. Arran's striking physical features, which attracted James Hutton and later followers or rival theorists to that island, are of a grander nature, but Bute at least can match the pattern of contrast between the Highland formations in the north and the Lowland formations in the south, and can supply its own quota of exceptions, apparent contradictions, and unsolved problems for the expert.

The northern half of Bute, with the Loch Fad valley marking the division, is predominantly metamorphic, mainly folded and contorted schists and schistose grits, with a continuous belt of grey and grey-blue slate formation. Those Dalradian rocks of Bute are the continuation of those across the water in Cowal, and field study has indicated that the broad belt of phyllites between Kames and Ettrick Bay is the same as the one between Dunoon and Loch Striven on the mainland.

The southern half of the island consists of red sandstone, over-laid in some places—for instance, at Ascog Hill and South Kilchattan—by trap rock. The Bute sandstone is sometimes referred to as 'old red sandstone', but James Kay in one of the many excellent papers published in the *Transactions of the Buteshire Natural History Society*, pointed out that, although one authority, Dr Bryce, had thought that the lowest band might belong to the Old Red Sandstone period, another expert, Professor Geikie, classed it with the lower carboniferous formation.

The Great Highland Fault is the dominating feature, with the valley of Loch Fad consequently providing one of the island's most interesting geological sections, where the transition from grey slate rocks to sandstone and conglomerate formations can be observed clearly. Incidentally the depth of the loch—36ft, and very much deeper than the present outlet—provides interesting evidence of probable ice movement. The smoothly rounded boulders and portions of grey rock, built up in unusual formation near Bardarroch Wood on the east side of the valley, also give indication of debris resulting from glacial change.

In this area the contrasting rocks and soils of north and south can be seen clearly, but a few apparent contradictions remain to provide mysteries for solving. At the end of the valley, close to the northern shore of Scalpsie Bay stands a rocky mound, 25ft high and approximately 20ft in diameter, known as The Haystack, and composed of Old Red Sandstone breccia. Obviously this should not be on the northern side of the fault where the rocks are igneous, but on the southern side where they are sedimentary.

Another major problem is raised by the existence of a large patch of columnar sandstone at the extreme southern end of the island, near Kilchattan Bay. This columnar sandstone outcrops on the shore and the raised beach cliff near the end of the road from Kilchattan pier. The columns, varying in size to a maximum of 7in in diameter, are at approximately right-angles to the bedding. The presence of a weathered dyke indicates a probable cause of the columnar development. The vertical columns, which show the crystalline form produced by fire, are in two beds, one above the other, but surprisingly separated by a bed of red sandstone nearly 2ft thick.

In the Dunagoil area, at the extreme south-west of the island, the basalt cliffs and pillow lava provide interesting resemblances to Ireland's Giant's Causeway.

The island has many trap-dykes caused by molten basalt from a volcano being forced up through a crack on the earth's surface. A striking example of the results of trap-rock cooling occurred at Whin Dike between Ascog and Kerrycroy, where the cliff in front of the sandstone rose perpendicular to a height of over 30ft, before quarrying at the beginning of this century spoiled the effect.

The only dyke in Bute with the characteristics of an old red sandstone intrusion occurs at the north-east corner of the Bull Loch in the hills above Rhubodach, and is similar to examples in Cowal, and near Colintraive. Carboniferous dykes are numerous, with well exposed examples near Bruchag Point and at Stravannan Bay. Composite dykes can be seen at Stravannan and Kerrytonlia Point.

Other interesting features include the layers of conglomerate at Craigmore and Ascog, the volcanic agglomerate at Kilchattan, the many small volcanic necks at the south end of the island, and the deposit of red clay below Little Grenach farm. Among minerals found in the necks and lavas are garnets, agates, chalcedony, and jasper, the Dunagoil area being a fruitful source.

Little commercial advantage has been taken of the Bute rocks, an exception being the use of local quarrystone in building Rothesay pier. Bute slates were used for buildings on the mainland in medieval times. The oldest remaining house in Glasgow, Provan's Lordship, built in 1471, was roofed with these small blue slates, which are considered too small and soft for modern use. For short spells at different periods these northern slates were quarried at various places, and were probably last worked in a 10ft thick seam at the beginning of this century. Expert opinion in 1946 advised that it would be uneconomic to reopen the quarries.

As early as 1663, and subsequently in 1758, attempts were made to exploit coal seams at Ascog. These were largely unsuccessful, and more recent explorations at the same site in

1903 and 1907 yielded no better results. The only stones now quarried in Bute are for roadmaking.

During the Ice Age Bute was covered by ice flowing from the north, and the main relics of this period are boulder clay and glacial striae. In two regions conspicuous dry valleys, according to W. J. McCallien writing in *The Rocks of Bute*, may have been formed by the meltwater of the ice. One of these lies to the east of St Blane's Chapel, and the other between Dhu Loch and the Ardscalpsie road. Glenmore, near Ettrick Bay, offers a good example of a U-shaped glacial valley.

The island of Bute has figured prominently in late-glacial and post-glacial research, and James Smith of Jordanhill was a pioneer in the study of arctic clays along the coasts of the Kyles of Bute. During excavations at the old Rothesay gasworks in 1854, discoveries in this field aroused the interest of the famous geologist Hugh Miller. Fine examples of late-glacial and post-glacial shell beds can be seen in Balnakaile Bay.

These marine clays are the low water deposits of the sea, which in other parts of the island deposited sand gravels at about 100ft above the present sea level. This raised beach is best seen between Kilchattan and Ettrick, but traces were discovered at Townhead, Rothesay, during gravel-removing operations. However, the most prominent raised beach in Bute is much more recent, belonging to the post-glacial period, rising to approximately 25ft, and extending all round the coast of the island. In places it is backed by high sea cliffs, with several examples of old sea caves, most notably the one at Dunagoil, which shows a marked resemblance to Fingal's Cave in Staffa.

Examples of erratics, where boulders were carried by glaciers at the end of the Ice Age, can be seen standing on the old red sandstone near Kerrycroy, and also at Ettrick Bay.

In general the island of Inchmarnock has the same geological characteristics as North Bute.

GEOGRAPHY

The main geographical features of the island were described in the introductory chapter, and the effects of the geological structure, and in particular the results of the last Ice Age on the varied and impressive scenery, have been noted. North Bute's close proximity to Argyll is a matter of terrain as well as distance. This part of the island shares the larger county's wild landscape of moor, hill, and bog, and, as it extends over a third of Bute's total area, it is obviously a significant factor.

Although the ferry crossing route from Rhubodach to Colintraive is the direct connection, the passage across the Narrows at the Burnt Islands marks the narrowest span of water. The whole of the area southward from the Kyles of Bute to the Ettrick plain is barren moorland, except for a very narrow coastal strip.

North Bute gives way suddenly to a fertile valley of rich sandy soil and extensive cultivation. This middle region of numerous farms, gentle hills, and small lochs, is the broadest part of the island, and also the most populated. The wide sandy stretch of Ettrick Bay on the west, and the deep sheltered bight of Rothesay Bay, together with the smaller bay of Port Bannatyne on the east, form natural boundaries. Running down the centre is a broad patch of moorland, extending from Barone Hill southward by way of Dhu Loch, while below this summit lies the well marked Highland Fault division, with Loch Fad prominent.

Farther to the south the pattern of well equipped farms in rich agricultural land continues, with the coastal areas most fertile. This gently undulating region extends by way of Bruchag and Kilchattan on the east, and Stravannan, Kingarth, and Dunagoil on the west, reaching towards the southernmost limits of Garroch Head, where the land rises to a plateau above steep slopes.

The differing nature of the soil in these main regions is

24

important economically as well as geographically. In the north the soil is acid, and the resultant vegetation is of the moorland type with very few trees. The central area has rich sandy soil, while the southern half of the island has predominantly the good light loam typical of the old red sandstone formation. Advantages can be seen in the amount of land easily workable in winter, the excellent grass, and the possibility of early crops, notably the Epicure potatoes, which can be harvested before the middle of June.

There are no mountains comparable to the neighbouring Arran ranges, the highest point on the north of the island being Windy Hill, rising to 914ft, while Barone Hill, which dominates the central valley, is 530ft, and the southern escarpment beyond Kilchattan 517ft.

CLIMATE

As indicated, the climate is temperate in every sense, and variations over the years are remarkably slight. The island's weather is exceptionally well documented, two organisations being mainly responsible. The old cotton mills kept continuous records of weather and rainfall during the entire period from 1800 to 1875, an achievement claimed to be the longest continuous meteorological observation in this country; and last century's pioneering work by the mills was followed up this century by Buteshire Natural History Society. Despite the difficulties of such an enterprise the records have been kept with consistent regularity and accuracy. In particular the continuous records during the periods 1915–24, 1945–55 and 1962–8 have great interest and value.

Some interesting details emerge from all sets of figures. Rainfall statistics have particular significance as they appear to show a definite trend. The cotton mills' records show that the average rainfall over the years from 1800 to 1875 was 48·56in, while the Natural History Society's record for the thirty years from 1939 to 1968 was 53·4in, and indeed during the ten-year period between 1945 and 1955 was as high as 55·6in. Up to the present no one appears to have investigated these figures, or suggested a possible cause for what amounts to a sizeable increase in annual rainfall. It would be interesting to know if this tendency applies over a wider stretch of western Scotland.

Of course, variations are notorious in an area of changeable climate—in the period mentioned rainfall annual totals rose as high as 70·18in, and fell as low as 47·26in, these two extremes coming in successive years! Nevertheless over the long period of records the increased average must have some significance. The wettest months are usually in autumn, and the driest in spring. The early summer months are almost invariably the sunniest; the first half of winter tends to be mild and damp, and the second half usually much colder. But, as in most parts of Scotland, there are frequent sudden changes and surprising contrasts. There is no month of the year when it is not possible to have a warm sunny day. Even midwinter can produce the occasional radiant day of sunshine and mildness, while a week in July or August may bring a spell of chilling rain with never a blink of sun. This phenomenon is usually attributed, according to native prejudice, to the onset of Greenock holidays, Glasgow Fair fortnight, or English Bank Holiday.

VEGETATION

The widely varied landscape of Bute encourages a great variety of vegetation. Few regions can have such richness and such contrasts in so small an area. Geography and climate are jointly responsible for the presence of palm trees, fuschias, and exotic plants round Rothesay Bay, and the botanical profusion of the south seems a world away from the comparative barren regions of the northern half of the island. The contrast, and the balance, have such interest, that it is to be hoped that the dangers of overspreading bracken on the one hand, and the effects of pesticides or pollution on the other, may be avoided.

Trees and flowers, hedgerow and meadow are bountiful in Bute; and while the birds thrive on the elderberries, haws, rowans, and other wild fruits of the island, the children gather brambles, raspberries, rose hips, and hazel nuts. Before the birds have built their nests, the children have started picking wood anemones and primroses, then mayflowers, marsh marigolds, wild hyacinth and campion. The yellow of the gorse is there to stain the Easter eggs, while the long stems of the silken broom, together with the beech branches, form the green and gold of May. The white drift of the jagged blackthorn, an early delight in spring, is followed by the abundant and sweet-scented hawthorn.

During the summer months Bute Natural History Society displays in the Museum successive gatherings of wildflowers currently in bloom, an idea of great educational interest to local schoolchildren, and also an advantage to visitors, who may note a sprig of St John's wort, a variety of orchis, comfrey, or yellow horned poppy, and discover where these can be found— by Loch Fad, the moors, or Scalpsie Bay.

The soil of Bute has no chalk and very little lime; indeed, shells from the Skerrol Shore used to be collected to improve the farm ground. On high land above the bracken, heather flourishes, with cotton grass, juniper, Scottish bluebell or harebell, lesser tway blade, cinquefoil, and occasionally the scarlet pimpernel. Among the flowers of the marshes are the spotted orchis, lousewort, butterwort, sundew, grass of Parnassus, lesser butterfly orchis, water lobelia, and sphagnum moss. Down nearer the sea are the sea blite, glasswort, sow thistle, butterwort, scurvy grass, thrift, scabious, butterbur, sea plantain, bulbous buttercup, gypsywort, and common skullcap. Sea purslane and lesser skullcap grow in the shingle beds near Ardscalpsie. At Bruchag Point the centaury and field felwort can be found, at Dunagoil the brookweed and beaked tassel pondweed, and at Millhole by Ascog the water plantain and marsh pennywort. Around the shores grow the bulrush and yellow iris.

Yellow too are the waterlilies that grow on Loch na Leigh, and the wild mimulus at the north end of the Kirk Dam. The bog bean grows on Loch na Leigh and white waterlilies on the Greenan Loch, together with the crowfoot much eaten by swans. Sweet Cicely is white in the hedgerows on the road to Wester Kames, and on the road to Dunagoil the hill is pink with spring beauty. There is a spread of hound's tongue by the ruined croft of Glen Callum on Garroch Head. Foxglove, harebell, and bell heather flourish on the old red sandstone, and honeysuckle riots over the hedgerows that shelter the herb robert and lesser celandine. Cranesbill can be seen at Dunagoil, purple among the rocks, with the purple-leaved orache and the little stone-crop. By the roadside is woodruff, lady's bedstraw, willow herb and knapweed, and farther in the woods in spring are ransoms, garlic, enchanter's nightshade, lesser wintergreen, wood sorrel, and frail anemone. The primroses are rich by Loch Fad, but perhaps most glorious of all in the naturally wooded slopes of the Kilmichael Road. Hazel, elder, birch, and blackthorn, are to be found there, with ash, hawthorn and willow, and a grove of oak trees. Oak is also present in the mixed woodland above Kilchattan Bay, with sycamore, ash and elder. In the wood behind the bay are many birches, but some are being destroyed by bracket fungi, and clearing has started. The birches at Achamore wood are carrying 'witches broom', another fungus. Some of the plantings have been cut down here, but there are still Douglas firs beyond Woodend House, and plantings of larch throughout the island, plus many little clumps of alder. Sycamore and beech grow in several areas, there have been a couple of spectacular plane trees on the island, and around

28

Rothesay are the elm trees. No elms grow from seed on Bute—the elms in front of the castle were planted by Lord Bute in 1875. There were also two famous old ash trees known as 'Adam and Eve' that stood on either side of the avenue below the High Church, and when the second was removed in 1904 it was estimated to be 257 years old; it was thought that at one time they might have flanked the southern approach to the Castle grounds.

It seems natural that an island owing much of its attraction to the hedges of beech and hawthorn, tended by the Bute estate, should shelter its most remarkable trees in the grounds of Mount Stuart House. The planting there started in 1718, and the work was continued by the third Earl of Bute, who took an active part in developing Kew Gardens. He planted most of the old trees that grow in the arboretum, and was also concerned with the Botanical Gardens in Edinburgh. In his grounds at Mount Stuart were planted oak, cedar of Lebanon, Spanish chestnut, Scots fir, beech, silver fir, and cork oak. Terrible storms, especially those of 1883 and 1884, levelled around 2,000 of the old trees, and hundreds were planted to fill the gaps—silver firs, redwood, and Douglas fir. The first Douglas fir to be planted in Bute must now be about 100 years old. The storms of 1968 again caused extensive damage, blowing down over 250 trees that are still being cleared away, but the beauty of the grounds survives. Besides the firs, there is a magnificent avenue of limes. In Kames Castle grounds are oaks, elm, beech and Spanish chestnut, but the largest oak tree on Bute was Kean's oak in the grounds of Woodend House, which the famous actor hoped would cover his grave. Although that plan was unfulfilled, the beautiful South American evergreen, *Araucaria Intricata*, is still on the lawn in front of the house, the whole setting as idyllic and peaceful as in Kean's most romantic imaginings.

Palm trees at Craigmore and Ardbeg bear witness to the mild climate, as in a smaller way does the fuschia. We are told by old inhabitants that the Skipper and Skeoch woods flanking Rothesay Bay were dense with trees before they were felled for timber in World War I. With the passage of time the tangle of woodland that has sprung up is still a very pleasant place to walk, and gives shelter to the birds.

Ferns grow in the walls of the causeway at Loch Fad, and in the ruins of St Blane's, while in the rock crevices of the cliffs at Dunagoil are the sea spleenwort and pennywort. Periwinkles and anemones can be found under the ledges by the shore, besides a wide variety of sea plants. The total list is extensive and impressive. On a day in June one naturalist noted ninety-three different plants in a 3 mile walk. No wonder the children of Bute continue to gather the wildflowers of the island.

ANIMALS

Animal life on Bute is unspectacular, showing very little difference from the pattern of Argyll and the west mainland. A significant feature, however, is the existence of roe deer, as this is one of the very few Scottish islands where the species can be found. These animals may be seen on several of the more remote regions of Bute.

Dr J. A. Gibson in his account of the *Mammals of Bute*, published in the 1970 *Transactions of Buteshire Natural History Society*, points out that although the Dunagoil excavations produced evidence of roe deer, they had become extinct and only returned about the middle of the nineteenth century; either they were deliberately introduced, or they may have swum across the Kyles, tempted by the new plantations. He also reports that during the 1930s at least thirty to forty were killed every year to reduce damage to young plantations. Single specimens of red deer are very occasionally reported on the northern parts of the island.

There are two small herds of wild goats on Bute, one at the north end and one at the south. All other large mammals have disappeared, but in excavations the bones of Celtic shorthorn, wild boar, Turbary sheep, and great fossil ox, have been found, a complete skeleton of the latter being discovered in clay pits at Kilchattan.

There were foxes, too, in ancient times, but none today, although the occasional individual may make a rare appearance. Bute has no badgers, but otters are common around the shores and by inland waters. They are also frequently seen on Inchmarnock and the Burnt Islands. As in Bute, Inchmarnock has the wild cat, gone feral. One of the boys on the island at present has a kitten with beautiful markings, which was born wild, but there are no true wild cats there or on Bute. It is still common across the water in Argyll, and the Dunagoil excavations prove the former existence of a larger race of wild cat.

Red squirrels were introduced in 1872 but have since died out, and there are no grey squirrels. Common mammals are the hedgehog, mole, stoat, weasel, hare, and brown rat. Rabbits, which were first introduced to Bute in 1835 but almost completely wiped out by myxomatosis by 1954, are returning, and the mountain hare is sighted now and again on the north of the island. Of the smallest animals the bank vole and field vole are common in Bute, and the water vole is declared to be 'not uncommon in suitable places'. The pygmy, common and water shrew are widely distributed.

Water bats have been seen in early evening on Loch Fad and other lochs, but there has been no certain record of Daubenton's bat. The long-haired bat is fairly common, and found everywhere, and the pipistrelle bat, which is common on Bute, is also present on Inchmarnock and has been observed flying between the two islands.

The coastal waters around Bute hold an interesting collection of sea animals. Seals are common around the Kyles area, Dunagoil, and Inchmarnock, where pups have occasionally been seen. Gibson reported two grey seals seen south of Garroch Head in 1967. One of the few recorded walrus seen around

Scotland, and the only one for the Clyde area, was noted in 1884 at Ettrick Bay by Professor Kerr, a Glasgow Professor of Zoology, but whales and dolphins are seen regularly in the sound of Bute. Porpoises and basking sharks provide interest and entertainment for visitors on summer cruises around the island and nearby sea-lochs, numbers varying considerably from year to year. In these exciting waters there have been individual sightings of white-beaked dolphin, bottle-nosed whale, and killer whale.

Butterflies are rich in Bute, but their range, as that of insects, varies little from other areas of the west coast. Huge nests of wood ants are prominent in the north of the island, each nest supporting as many as 100,000 ants, whose tracks spread out in different directions and extend over 70yd.

REPTILES

Bute's list of reptiles contains little of surprise or outstanding interest. It is perhaps noteworthy that there are no adders or grass-snakes, although there have been occasions when specimens have been brought to the island, and over the years unconfirmed sightings have been reported. Slow-worms and common lizards are fairly common. Toads, frogs, and newts are represented. J. A. Gibson, in addition to his list of mammals, has compiled a list of Bute's reptiles, and his up-to-date report is published in the 1970 Buteshire Natural History *Transactions*.

BIRDS

Bute is a remarkable area for bird life, being unusually rich in both residents and visitors, while the range of seabirds, in particular, is most extensive. This diversity was indicated by the count published by J. M. McWilliam over 40 years ago, in which he listed 168 observations—possibly a slightly exaggerated total, as up to forty of these sightings were exceptional rather than typical, but nevertheless an impressive record.

McWilliam's study has been carried on by J. A. Gibson, a naturalist who is a most worthy successor, while the work of Dorothy Marshall, with the help of Natural History Society members and Junior Naturalists, has provided valuable data on the changing pattern of bird life on the island. Continued observations and counts, together with up-to-date check lists, have outlined the present-day pattern. On the whole, the changes, though occasionally striking (for instance, in eider duck numbers), are small against the general pattern, and the ornithologist will be encouraged to realise that, despite the encroaching attacks of modern civilisation, Bute's bird life retains an abundance and variety rarely matched in such an easily accessible area. Even the Clyde seabird disaster of September 1969, though disturbing and distressing in some respects, has been shown by J. A. Gibson to have been matched by similar disasters in 1859, 1872, 1889, 1913, 1941, and 1948.

When McWilliam took his count of Bute birds in the 1920s, he noted that there were twenty birds for every resident on the island. It would be an interesting ploy for the visitor to make his own count, for there is still an astonishing variety of birds to be found, and the species listed in 1969 have changed very little from the earlier records. The earliest record of all was the breast-bone of a goose, the size of a pink-footed goose, found together with the bone of a greenfinch, and one of a rook or crow, during the excavation of the caves at Dunagoil, dating back to Mesolithic times. And one of the most recent records tells of a pink-footed goose leaving a flock of greylag geese, attaching itself to three or four farm geese frequenting the estuary of the Quochag Burn, and remaining there for some time.

Certainly the thousands of greylag geese and wigeon that visit Bute early in October each year, and leave before the end of April, are a familiar sight on the sand flats of Kilchattan Bay, or on the fields beside St Ninian's Bay. Other winter migrants

33

include the brent goose, purple sandpiper, grey plover, bar- and black-tailed godwits, turnstones, waxwings, bramblings, fieldfares, redwings, water rail, goldeneye, pintail and common pochard ducks, and whooper swans. The red-breasted merganser is very common in the neighbourhood of Bute, and can be seen in winter and early spring, swimming and diving in Rothesay Bay and in the fresh water of the Greenan Loch. The great northern diver is comparatively common in the Firth till late in the spring. The tufted duck and shoveler frequent the Greenan Loch, and the goldeneye is a regular winter and spring visitor to Loch Ascog. Shelduck, mallard, teal and eider breed locally, and the eider-duck colony has increased over the years. McWilliam writes that it has 'now begun to breed on the Clyde', but now the birds and their young, swimming off the shores of the island, are a familiar and gentle part of early summer. Dorothy Marshall's surveys and counts of 1968 and 1969 record over 200 families.

Although the winter migrating birds are an exciting sight, the visitor's special interest is with the birds that stay over the summer, and whether he sails over the ferry from the north with the swans, or by the larger boat from the open Firth with the gannets from Ailsa Craig, he will be aware of them before he lands. Feeding the gulls on the Clyde steamers used to be a tourist's pastime, and six of the species of gulls that nest in Britain are to be seen in great numbers on the shores of Bute: the great black-backed, lesser black-backed, herring, black-headed, common, and kittiwake. The common tern is a summer visitor, although there is a slow decrease in its numbers; the arctic tern is not uncommon, and the optimist can hope for the return of the roseate tern, as the first known to science was shot on the wee 'Eilans' in Millport Bay, and there were recordings of them on the Clyde until 1969. Still more rare are the records of the glaucous gull and Icelandic gull, both sighted and shot at Port Bannatyne in the past. Skuas have been seen; razorbills nest on Ailsa Craig and can be seen easily around Bute. There

Page 35 (above) Rothesay Castle: the circular fortress, built on a mound at the edge of the sea, was prominent in Scottish history from the twelfth until the seventeenth century; (below) this view from the north-west shows the palace built by King James IV, and one of the original circular towers

Page 36 (*above left*) The Marquess of Bute and family: the present Marquess continues in the family tradition as a conservationist, but also takes an active part in Bute's modern enterprises; (*above right*) the Norman arch of St Blane's: the twelfth century arch divides the chancel from the nave of the two chamber church built on the site of an earlier Celtic chapel; (*below*) Kames castle: the seat of the Bannatyne family built in the fourteenth century and although extensively altered is one of the oldest continuously inhabited houses in Scotland

used to be a huge puffin colony on Ailsa Craig, but few nest there now. Cormorant, shag, southern guillemot, and smaller numbers of black guillemot, have all been spotted and indiscriminately termed 'dookers' by children on boats and piers of the Clyde.

Waders share the sandy bays of the island with the paddling children, oystercatchers, curlews, and ringed plovers, running before the happy invaders. The common sandpiper nests near the sea, and the common redshank breeds in numbers on marshy ground near the shore. The greenshank has been seen, as have the sanderling, knot, and little stint. A few pairs of the southern dunlin nest on Bute, and of course the little turnstone is found practically in every month of the year, although it breeds in the north. The estuary of the Pointhouse Burn is a favourite spot.

Beyond the sand are the marshy stretches loved by ducks, and mouths of burns haunted by waders. The freshwater lochs —Greenan, Quien, Ascog, and Fad—are full of weed and teeming with birds, teal, wigeon, the little moorhen, coot and little grebe. Mallards nest on the hillsides adjacent to the Quien, and year after year a pair of mute swans have nested on the crannog there. Bewick's swan has been seen on Loch Fad and the Greenan. Although the heronries have gone from Kingarth, Loch Fad and Rhubodach, a few herons can be seen around the Kyles of Bute and at Ettrick. The little Loch na Leigh on the south end of the island carries the same variety of water birds, although it was particularly noted for its black-headed gull colony.

On higher ground by the Dhu Loch near Barone Hill, and the Bull Loch in the north end of the island, the birds of the moors—black grouse and red grouse—are found. The nightjar nests yearly in the hills close to the Dhu Loch, and its 'bubbling' or 'churring' note can be heard in the still air. The ring ouzel has been seen near the Dhu Loch and the Bull Loch. In the north end of the island the golden plover breeds on the moors,

C

at an altitude of 400ft and upwards. The remote hills of north Bute can be very rewarding for the bird watcher. Peregrine falcons and ravens are known to have nested there. Hen harriers are seen from time to time. A pair with young were seen in July 1969, as were merlins, and an osprey was sighted over the Kyles of Bute in 1967. Of course, it may have been on its way to Loch Garten! Buzzards certainly nest on Bute and can be seen both in the north and south ends of the island. Kestrels are fairly common, but sparrowhawks have been decreasing, although the fact that they have been added to the protected list, and that insecticides are being watched, may help the situation. The common snipe is more fortunate, if not perhaps reaching McWilliam's standards: 'I have never, even in Ireland seen a place where snipe are more numerous at all seasons than in Bute. Great numbers breed on the island. Without especially looking for their nests I have seen four or five in a day'. From his own garden at Craigmore the naturalist could watch the 'evening love-flight' of the woodcock in early summer, a bird that also nested in considerable numbers on the island and can still be seen. Beyond Craigmore, on the shore road to Kingarth, through the Bute Estate, the pheasants stroll in the early evening, and the common partridge is abundant everywhere.

Over the years the changes in the pattern have been slight. The rook roost described by McWilliam in the *Scottish Naturalist* of 1923 has only moved a little farther south, and Dorothy Marshall's report of a 1969 count shows similar repetitions. Thousands of rooks still gather near Loch Ascog in winter, coming in from their feeding grounds in Cowal, Ayrshire, Renfrew and Argyll. The largest rookery is in the Foley Woods. It seems that the rooks have always been heard around the High Street, in whatever trees were available to them. The tawny owl, too, seeks out any suitable planting, and the barn owl must accommodate itself to slight changes. Only the short-eared owl seems to have given up, for it has not been seen since 1966 on Scoulag Moor. But the cuckoo sings every spring, the lapwings wheel over the farm fields, and the corncrake or landrail has only slightly shifted its ground to make way for housing development. It used to call at night above the old quarry at Chapelhill, and was also heard near Kilchattan Bay. McWilliam reported rock doves as sleeping in the caves at Dunagoil, and that is still the place to look for them. Collared doves are seen quite frequently, and the woodpigeon is common.

Bute is fairly well wooded, with a variety of trees, and those woods and shrubberies shelter a large number of small birds—the blue tit, great tit, and less frequently the cole tit and long-tailed tit. Goldcrest, tree creeper, willow warbler, wood warbler, and spotted flycatcher are all present, with finches, especially the greenfinch, great spotted woodpecker, siskin, twite, lesser redpoll, blackbird, thrush, robin, wren and sparrow. The cross-bill has been seen on pines above Craigmore, and out on the open ground among the gorse bushes are the whinchat, chiff-chaff, British stonechat, wheatear, corn bunting, linnet, yellowhammer, meadow pipit and rock pipit. As with the snipe, McWilliam knew of 'no place where the rock-pipit is more common than in Bute'. In the reeds and rushes the sedge-warbler sings. It is attracted to willows on the little island on Loch na Leigh, an island that is a floating mass of tangled roots. The reed bunting can be found near the shore at Kingarth, Kerrycroy, and at Loch Fad and Ettrick. The blackcap inhabits the same terrain and the skylark climbs to the sky there. In early evening the swifts and swallows dive for their supper, and the sandmartin can be seen close to Loch Ascog where there is a sandy bank suitable for nesting. Like the rook and jackdaw the starling crosses to the mainland in the morning and returns before dark. There is a record of a rose-coloured starling seen in 1925.

If Bute sometimes seems like the Island of Birds of the Saint's voyages, it is right to remember Inchmarnock, an island that perhaps has a better historical claim to the title. There is a great congestion of gulls' nests at the south end, and many

39

eider and mallard share their site, besides nesting elsewhere on the island. On the west side kestrels nest. Rock doves, curlews, oystercatchers, ringed plovers, redshank, woodcock, snipe, common sandpipers and shelduck are regular nesters, and can be easily observed by the visitor to the island. The little Burnt Islands in the Kyles of Bute support a fair number of nesting birds—common gulls, herring gulls, lesser black-backs and great black-backs, oystercatchers, eider ducks, and mute swans. Others known to have nested in these islets are red-breasted merganser, moorhen, sandpiper, arctic tern, and reed bunting. On one occasion a hen pheasant was encountered with seven chicks, but she was maybe on her holidays! Bute is an early island for birds as well as crops, and the swallows had settled in by Loch Fad on 16 April 1972.

Although every bird watcher will be seeking to add rare birds to his list of sightings, in the hope that the rarely recorded—the rose-coloured starling, the mealy redpoll, or the short-eared owl—will turn up again, the resident on Bute will always delight in the flights of well known birds in well loved places—rooks above the High Street on a winter afternoon, skylarks singing their hearts out above Ettrick on a summer morning, swallows darkening the approach to Kilmichael Farm in the evening, lapwings wheeling, curlews rising, snipe wings beating over the Westlands, and always the gulls, ferrying to and fro across the Clyde.

3 PREHISTORY & ANCIENT HISTORY

AFTER the ice-cap that covered Scotland during the Pleistocene period had receded, several centuries elapsed before the first men came to the country, possibly around 4000 BC. The early food-gatherers of the Middle Stone Age were probably visitors rather than settlers, coming from the sea and staying for the summer only. They were cave-dwellers and primitive hunters, whose settlements and 'kitchen-middens' have been found in several parts of Scotland. Little trace of them can be seen in Bute, but beneath the Neolithic burial cairn at Glecknabae on the old sea beach, which is about 25ft higher and 150yd away from the present shore, is an example of a shell-mound or kitchen-midden, probably of this period, and indicating a possible site of a Mesolithic camp.

Disappointingly, Bute's caves provide little evidence of this period. An extensive survey by local archaeologist Dorothy Marshall in 1936 revealed deposits of shells but nothing to date the shell layers. With the coming of the next influx of travellers from southern lands Bute probably received her first true settlers; from this Neolithic period onwards the island has a continuous and remarkably well documented history, and there is ample evidence that settlements in Bute were inhabited well before 2000 BC.

Being an island at the centre of the early water-routes, Bute was visited by successive waves of Neolithic men who brought from the south their knowledge of agriculture and introduced the first domestic animals. From 2500 BC these New Stone Age men appear to have lived in various parts of the island, but although relics of this period are plentiful, the actual villages are difficult to locate. One of the comparatively rare domestic sites, and, indeed, as Professor Stuart Piggott has pointed out, one of the few known inhabited Neolithic sites in Scotland, was found at Townhead, Rothesay. Excavations produced polished stone axes, pottery similar to that found at Orkney's Skara Brae, nut shells, and perhaps the most remarkable find—a grain of wheat to prove the existence of farming. An even earlier site is to be seen near the vitrified fort at Dunagoil. The presence of a ruined Megalithic chamber without a cairn suggests this may be the oldest site on the island. In a nearby cave fragments of Neolithic pottery have been found.

There is plentiful evidence of the period in the presence of burial chambers unsurpassed anywhere in Scotland. In various parts of the island these ancient burial cairns and chambers, with the accompanying assortment of querns, pots, stone axes, and other relics of the Neolithic period, help to build up a picture of the life and death of the first dwellers in Bute.

Chambered cairn burials provide valuable clues in tracing the movements of the early people who came to Bute, and in 1903 Professor Bryce undertook the excavation of all the Neolithic and Bronze Age tombs known to exist on the island at that time, and used this experience when giving a paper on the prehistory of Bute to the Bute Natural History Society in 1909. Professor Bryce excavated the chambered cairns at Bicker's Houses to the west of the Dhu Loch in the hills above Loch Fad, finding relics, including a flint knife, fragments of urns, and some pieces of bone, which were sent to the National Museum of Antiquities in Edinburgh. He visited the ruined chambered cairn known as St Michael's Grave, at Kilmichael, finding fragments of bone and flint flakes, and also examined a long cairn with a ruined chamber at one end in Lenihuline wood. The latter, although perhaps the most impressive of the cairns, provided no relics.

42

Professor Bryce believed that the pieces of vessels found in Bute resembled examples found in France and the Pyrenees rather than those of Scandinavia, suggesting that these chamber-builders came from the south by way of the western coasts. Although he had excavated three of the four chambered tombs in north-west Bute, the most exciting of the four, Glenvoidean, did not yield its secrets until later investigations following its discovery by Mrs D. B. Taylor, who was also concerned with much of the digging during the period 1963–77. Glenvoidean is situated above Kilmichael Farm, close to St Michael's Grave, but on a higher contour, offering spectacular views across the Kyles of Bute to Argyll and Arran. It is officially dated c14 2900±150 (uncorrected), and is probably as old as 3200 BC. These extensive excavations over the past decade have been carried out by members of Buteshire Natural History Society, assisted by visiting archaeologists, students, and members of Bute Junior Naturalists. Bute is exceptionally lucky in having such an active and enthusiastic society, and the Glenvoidean enterprise is only one of its many contributions.

Miss Dorothy Marshall, who has been prominent in organising and supervising the Glenvoidean excavations, has published fascinating preliminary reports, including a study in the 1967 *Transactions*. A fuller description embodying details of recent 1971 excavations is in preparation. As Miss Marshall points out, it is seldom that a site of such richness has escaped previous recognition and investigation. One of the exciting finds was a group of three pots—one completely intact, the other two crushed but now restored—of Beacharra type ware, which have been given a date of approximately 2300 BC, indicating that the cairn was in use for at least 600 years.

A number of querns, several of which are on display in the Natural History Museum, have been found on the island, providing interesting evidence of the development of corn-grinding methods used by these first Neolithic farmers.

The successors of the later New Stone Age men worked with bronze, and it appears likely that their customs and culture were superimposed on the chambered-cairn people. As few domestic sites of this period have been discovered, knowledge of the Bronze Age in Bute relies mainly on burial sites, and, as Professor Bryce has pointed out, an interesting feature of the island's archaeology is the clear evidence provided of the meeting of the chambered-cairn and short-cist cultures.

In 1903 Professor Bryce discovered a cist in a cairn at Scalpsie Bay containing burnt human bones, indicating the new idea of cremation. The presence here of a flint knife showed that flint instruments had not been discarded, but fresh features included a richly ornamented bronze urn, a bronze pin, and lignite beads. An approximate dating gave the period as around 1600 BC.

Another grave of the same type had been discovered at Mount Stuart in 1887. This cist contained a skeleton in a crouched position, the arms and legs being flexed. There was also a splendid necklace of lignite beads and a distinctive food vessel, which are on show in Edinburgh. It should be noted that in Bute as in other parts of western Scotland the urns are mainly of the food-vessel type rather than the beaker type common on the east coast of Scotland.

In 1933 a group of three cists were found at Little Kilmory, yielding bronze fragments and a food vessel, and in 1952 a Middle Bronze Age cist was discovered at Kildavanan. Perhaps the most impressive discovery took place in 1958 when eighteen cists were found under a 25ft high cairn at Rullecheddan Farm, but although some urns were unearthed, no scientific record is available.

In 1961 there was an important discovery on Bute's offshore island of Inchmarnock. On the north end of this small island,

44

one of a group of three cists, beautifully constructed, when opened revealed the skeleton of a young woman crouched on a bed of shingle with a flint knife and scattered beads of a necklace at her side. This lovely and now famous lignite collar, with its 135 beads restrung, is on view at the Natural History Museum in Rothesay, and attracts many admiring visitors. The Inchmarnock necklace, similar in some respects to the Mount Stuart collar, is one of less than sixty found, and, apart from being the largest, is a particularly fine example. An approximate date of 1500 BC has been given.

The stone circles at St Colmac's near Ettrick Bay, and the standing stones at Kingarth and Largizean are probably Bronze Age, dating perhaps to around 1500 BC. The strangely shaped large stones beside the Kingarth–Dunagoil road are clearly visible, since the woods have been cut down. The crannog on Quien Loch, with the 100ft causeway leading to it, is probably Late Bronze Age, or early Iron Age; and the remains of another example can be seen on the Dhu Loch. Traces of the civilisation occur at Little Dunagoil cave, which was occupied from the late Bronze Age to the medieval period.

IRON AGE

During the last century BC a fresh wave of settlers brought knowledge of new crafts from the continent, and these users of iron were responsible for a greatly changed way of life, involving improved tools, agricultural development, and the building of forts and strongholds. Bute has nearly a dozen of these Iron Age sites, most of them close to the shore. A typical example is at Scalpsie, where a fragment of bone comb was found during clearing in 1959. Dunallant Fort, near Ettrick Bay, is one of the largest forts on the island, and its ramparts can be clearly recognised, but the best known example is the vitrified fort at Dunagoil, the supreme example of its kind, richer than all the other Scottish Iron Age sites. Excavations have shown that the fort here and the cave below were occupied for 300 years by a well organised community; and have produced evidence enabling an authentic picture of life at that time to be built up.

Dunagoil's position on a high promontory above the beach allowed for a fortification provided partly by the precipice and partly by a constructed wall. The vitrified part of the wall has aroused conflicting theories on its possible origin—between those believing that vitrification was intentional, and the majority who are certain it was accidental. Large-scale excavations were organised in 1915, 1919, and 1925, and the results of these observations were printed in Bute Natural History Society's *Transactions*. It was found that the inside walls may have been as high as 15ft, and that the inhabitants lived in clay and wattle huts, working bronze and iron, using crucibles, an ore furnace, and bronze casting moulds. Bone was obviously used widely, rough pottery was made, and there were indications of weaving and jewellery-making.

The men of the time were hunters and fishers, sailors and craftsmen, who between them fashioned a way of community life that survived for several centuries.

Although the excavations at nearby Little Dunagoil, which were organised by the Bute Natural History Society in association with the Society of Antiquities of Scotland during the period 1958–62, covered a wider range than the immediate one, confirmation of linking with the larger Iron Age fort at Dunagoil was provided. The most interesting finding of these excavations was the proof of occupation from late Bronze Age right up to the thirteenth century. Apart from Bronze and Iron Age relics, traces of Dark Age and Celtic habitation were found, while the massive longhouses, with their characteristic Norse features, brought the record up to medieval times.

It is difficult to divide prehistory from history proper—in many respects there is more historical value in well documented archaeological evidence than early historical accounts based on conjecture as well as established fact. Scotland has had more than her share of instances where legend has been presented as factual record, and it would be illogical to expect that a small island like Bute could be sure that all the stories of the past were rooted in reality.

Despite the island's long period of human occupation there is a great lack of certain information about the early years. Indeed Ptolemy's maps give little clue to the existence of Bute, and the earliest written reference is in the *Annals of Tigherare* in the eleventh century, where reference is made to the monastic settlement of Kingarth. The names Rothesay and Bute, which became known soon after that time, were probably Norse in origin.

Several local historians have written the history of Bute, the most notable being J. K. Hewison's two-volume *The Isle of Bute in Olden Times*, published in 1893 and 1895; John Blain's *History of Bute*, published in 1880; and J. E. Reid's *History of the County of Bute*, published in 1864. Dorothy N. Marshall's excellent *History of Bute*, whose value is greatly enhanced by the author's expert archaeological knowledge, was prepared for Bute Museum and Buteshire Natural History Society in 1950, and has been revised and enlarged for subsequent new editions in 1964, 1967, 1969 and 1971. It is now recognised as the standard up-to-date archaeological and historical guide to the island.

Of the nineteenth-century books, Blain's, though not the first to be published, was certainly the earliest to be written, probably some years before 1820. Blain had come to Rothesay from Wigtownshire in 1761, and among his many posts on the island were those of chamberlain to the Marquess of Bute, town clerk of Rothesay, and sheriff clerk of Buteshire (which he held for many years). For half a century he was not only a prominent figure in public life, but had something of a monopoly in local government offices. There is a story, probably apocryphal, that when invitations were sent out from the mainland to the holders of several offices in Bute, Blain turned up at the function as occupier of all of them. Apart from his usefulness in public affairs, Blain certainly contributed to knowledge of his times through his well kept records, notes, and writings. He died in 1819 or 1820, and portions of the original manuscript of his history of Bute, which are in the possession of Bute Natural History Society, suggest that the date of composition might be around 1800. His style of writing is interesting, and it is known that J. E. Reid had access to Blain's manuscript, and drew from it for the first published history.

Incidentally Blain appears to have forestalled the local minister, who became known round the Firth of Clyde for his regular prayers for 'the inhabitants of Cumbrae and the adjacent islands of Great Britain and Ireland'. Blain wrote in his history: 'The islands of the Larger and Lesser Cumbray intervene between Bute and the Continent', and throughout the book he always refers to the Scottish mainland as the Continent.

Hewison is especially strong and expertly knowledgeable in his detailed descriptions of historical monuments, including Rothesay Castle and St Blane's Chapel, and although his earlier chapters perhaps rely too heavily on legend and conjecture, these are inevitable dangers in any attempt at a continuous story and reconstruction of an age so long past.

Archaeology, which has done so much to provide the vital clues to the way men lived and died in Neolithic, Bronze, and Iron Age times, sheds some light, too, on the Dark Ages and the coming of Celt and Viking. Crucibles and Celtic crosses from Dunagoil help to set the period of the early Christians, while the advent of the Vikings is recalled in sword hilts and tombstones.

THE COMING OF THE SAINTS

The keynote of the early Celtic Christian period is found in the saga of the amazing voyages of the first saints and missionaries who sailed the Scottish waters, setting up their centres and chapels on the islands and promontories of the western coast. Bute, firstly because of its position near the centre of these sea-routes, and secondly because of its own attractions of fertile land, gentle slopes, and natural sheltered bays and kyles, was visited by many of these pioneers.

Placenames give as good an idea as any of those early visitors. Ninian, Marnoc, Colmac, Catan and Blane are among those who have left name as well as ruins in many corners of the island. Ninian travelled from Rome to Galloway, where he built the first chapel at the Isle of Whithorn, and almost certainly he or his disciples in the course of further voyages set up the chapel at St Ninian's Point on the west of Bute.

St Ninian's Chapel, which lies at the end of a peninsula, near the village of Straad, and the nearest point to the isle of Inchmarnock, was excavated in 1952–4 by W. Glen Aitken. Discoveries of great interest were made, including an altar with a cavity that was probably used as a relic-holder. Apparently the place of worship and burial was built on the site of an early pagan burial ground, and probably dates back to the sixth or seventh centuries, certainly not later than the eighth century. (The site was abandoned after Viking raids of the eighth and ninth centuries.) Apart from its similar peninsular position to that of the Isle of Whithorn, several unique features suggest that it could have been a retreat relating to the main monastery in the same way as Physgill cave relates to Whithorn. There is certainly a link to support the theory that it could have been founded from Candida Casa.

The continuous chain of Christian teaching has been likened to the unbroken design of a Celtic cross, and there are fascinating but elusive links between the early saints. The aim of St Patrick was to carry the gospel to the remotest island and farthest valley of the north. The bishop who veiled St Brigid was his pupil, and some have thought that he may have been the saint associated with the church of Kilmichael in north Bute. There are two dedications to St Brigid herself—at Kilbride in the north, and

49

at St Bride's Hill, now called Chapelhill, in Rothesay. Only the name remains at Kilbride, but as late as 1830 an engraving shows the remains of St Bride's Chapel on Chapelhill, and there are records of fifteenth-century celebrations 'in the chapel of the blessed Brigid'.

The name of Brendan 'the navigator', surely the farthest travelled of the holy men, appears all round the western seas from Mount Brandon on the Dingle Peninsula, to Orkney, and to Brittany. His voyages were long, and inspired legendary tales of visits to islands of sheep, or flowers or birds. No chapel commemorates him on Bute, but he may have made landfall during his voyage round the western islands in the middle of the sixth century. Certainly the islanders who throughout the centuries have called themselves Brandanes have preserved the name, while Kilbrannan Sound suggests another connection.

Marnoc, whose name is also retained in the Ayrshire town of Kilmarnock, was said to have met St Columba in Dalriada while still a boy. A legendary account describes Columba's reply to a monk's rebuke of the boy for accosting him. 'Do not scold him, this one will be a great preacher.' Remains of St Marnoc's first monastic settlement can still be seen across the water on the little isle of Inchmarnock, together with Celtic crosses and evidence of old burials. Fragments of sculptured stone and shafts of crosses from the old chapel and burying ground can be seen in the Rothesay museum, and similar relics are still being discovered on the island.

Colmac and Catan, followers of the Irish church of Patrick, and forerunners of Columba, came to Bute, the former to establish a chapel north of Ettrick Bay, the latter to 'seek retirement in a cell near Kilchattan Bay'. The preaching cross on an earlier standing stone at East St Colmac is the only remaining sign of the chapel of Kilmachalmaig, a Celtic foundation that existed until well after the Reformation.

Catan, who was said to have been educated by Patrick,

'sought retirement' in Bute, making his cell at Kilchattan Bay, where village, well and hill still bear his name. Legend connects him with Blane, sometimes in uncle-nephew, sometimes pupil-tutor relationship.

Blane, who is also associated with Dunblane, Kilblain near Dumfries, Kilblane in Kintyre, and Strathblane, was believed to have been born in Bute in the sixth century, then educated in the monastic school of Bangor in Ireland before returning to his birthplace. He is noted as 'Blaan the mild of Cenngarad' in the Martyrology of Aengus—'Bishop of Cenn-garad—Dunblane is his chief city and he is of Cenn-garad in the Gall-Gaedala'—and certainly the genius that chose such a site for his monastery seems still 'Blaan the mild of Kingarth'. The ruined chapel, set in a green valley on the slopes above Dunagoil Bay at the south end of Bute, is sheltered from the winds yet open to a glorious view across the firth to Arran. St Blane's, now under the care of the Secretary of State, is the earliest actual monastic foundation on the island and is one of the best preserved Celtic sites in Britain. It is impossible to fix the exact date of the building of the monastery, but it was certainly in existence in 574, only eleven years after St Columba's settlement on Iona. There is clear evidence of Christian burial there in the sixth and seventh centuries, and also that the monastery became a cultural centre around that time. (A bronze casting of an eighth-century crucible was found, the only complete one in Scotland.)

St Blane's is mentioned in records as one of the great monasteries of the seventh century, and King Aidan's grandson is said to have been sent there to be educated. The names of all the eight abbots are recorded, from the first around 570 to the last around 790. The early monastery was independent of Iona, with Bangor for its parent house. According to the historian Bede: 'St. Columba had no more jurisdiction in Lismore, than he had in Applecross or Kingarth'.

In the eighth century the Vikings began their raids on the

western isles, and other dependent chapels on the island would be destroyed at the same time as St Blane's was. Eight years after the last abbot died in 790, the Norsemen raided and burned the monastery. The quiet land of St Blane's must have kept something of its mystery through the Dark Ages, to inspire the building of the little Norman church on the same spot, over the ruins of the first walls.

The present St Blane's chapel ruin is mainly twelfth century, with a good example of a Norman arch, but clear evidence of the earlier buildings remains. There were three walls, one enclosing the primitive buildings under the ridge, another taking in the present church, and the third forming a boundary to all the abbey lands 'from sea to sea'. Within the outer wall of the monastery stood the kitchen, dormitories, guesthouses for pilgrims, and workshops where farming and fishing tools could be made or repaired, and even ritual ornaments fashioned. The inner walls enclosed the consecrated ground and the chapel itself. The lower burial ground is traditionally known as the women's burial ground, and there may have been a small chapel there.

The practice of separate burial, followed for a period in the Celtic monasteries in Ireland, lasted for a long time at St Blane's, and the report of a Presbytery of Dunoon visit to Kingarth in 1661 referred to 'this superstitious custom of burying their men and women in two diverse churchyards', which was promptly tackled by the Presbytery passing an Act to end the custom.

The charter through which Alan the Steward disponed St Blane's Church to Paisley Abbey in 1204 defines the disposition as 'the church of Kengarf in the Isle of Bute, with all the chapels and with the whole jurisdiction of the same isle, and with the whole land which St Blaan, it is said formerly girded across country from sea even to sea, by boundaries secure and visible, so that freely and quietly as any church in the whole kingdom of Scotland it shall be held more free and peaceable'. Inciden-

52

Page 53 (*above*) Evening light on Port Bannatyne; the port, Bute's largest centre of population outside Rothesay, had two thousand inhabitants at the height of its development, and remains a popular holiday centre; (*left*) Wester Kames: the tall turreted keep was a good example of old Scottish architecture, but was reconstructed in 1905

Page 54 (*above*) St Blane's chapel and churchyard: St Blane's had been one of the great monasteries of the seventh century, while the later church was used for regular services until the eighteenth century; (*below*) Dunagoil fort and cave: Dunagoil vitrified fort is an outstanding iron age site, and together with the cave below was occupied for 300 years as a well-organised community

tally this is the first record of land ownership in Bute. Alan the Steward might have been responsible for the Norman addition to St Blane's church, when the eastern gable was pierced with two pointed windows and two lancet windows were inserted in the chancel walls. During the fifteenth century a double light window was added to the south wall and the nave was extended to the west.

Under the Cluniac order of Paisley, the livelier scene of the old Celtic community at St Blane's must have given way to a more silent austerity. The church remained under the jurisdiction of Paisley Abbey until the Reformation, and was used regularly for services until the early eighteenth century. Since that time the beautiful chapel has been left as a noble ruin, but in the true sense it remains a place of pilgrimage and worship.

Of the other dependent chapels destroyed by the Norsemen the walls of Kilmichael in north Bute still stand, but only the names remain at Kildavanan, and Crioslagmory (the site is still called the Chapel field, and Chapeltown on Loch Fad). There are remains at Cruiskland, about a mile north of St Ninian's Chapel, and at Kilmory on the hill south of Little Kilmory farm. There was a chapel to St Bride on St Bride's Hill, now Chapelhill, while Lady Kirk was probably built on the site of an earlier Celtic church.

The lovely little chapel of St Mary's can still be seen beside the present church at the top of the High Street in Rothesay. It was part of the old Cathedral of Sodor, the Bishopric of Man, once governed by the Celtic Church. It was transferred to the See of Nidaros in Norway by a papal bull in 1154. The *Chronicle of Man* states that 'Alan, a native of Galloway, ruled the Sodorian church honourably, died on the 15th. February 1320, and is buried in the church of the blessed Mary of Rothesay in Buth'. The next bishop, Gilbert, is buried 'in the said church of Both'.

The Norsemen, who had destroyed the earlier churches, came as raiders but later stayed as settlers. Traces of the Viking raids

D

during the last years of the eighth century and the early years of the ninth have been found in Bute, and by the following centuries their numbers had increased sufficiently to enable them to challenge for control of the island.

4   MEDIEVAL & MODERN HISTORY

THE circular fortress of Rothesay Castle, the main medieval monument on the island, was built on a mound close to the sea, and remained for many centuries not only the focal point for local history but also a prominent centre in the story of Scotland's national development. Even today it is an imposing building, with many interesting architectural features, but its position is less prominent now than when it was on the edge of the sea. Even 150 years ago, before harbour and promenade developments, the sea was only 75yd away.

THE VIKINGS

The castle is first specifically mentioned during the time of the Vikings, and an early record tells of the Norsemen in 1228 besieging the garrison of the Steward of Scotland. There is some reason to believe that the castle may have been founded by Magnus Barefoot, King of Norway, in 1098, as one of the fortresses erected in an endeavour to consolidate the Norse conquests of the western isles. An alternative theory is that the Scots built the castle as a frontier garrison against the Norsemen. Evidence is inconclusive, but the apparent means of construction suggest that, whoever was responsible, the date of building was towards the end of the eleventh century.

The Norsemen, like other early settlers, enjoyed the pastoral lands and sheltered bays of Bute, and even in their first raids left relics like the cross to Gutlief on Inchmarnock and the swastika cross at East Colmac. Thereafter the possession of Bute

57

was contested by Scot and Viking, and for two centuries the castle seems to have changed hands frequently. It was possibly under the control of Sigurd of Orkney before the Battle of Clontarf, probably reverting to the Scots for a few years under Malcolm II, then submitting again after the spectacular return of the Norsemen when Magnus Barefoot conquered the west in 1098.

Magnus is said to have made an arrangement with the Scottish king that all the isles of Scotland towards the setting sun, round which a ship might be steered, were to be ceded to Norway. He dramatically annexed extra land by steering his galley, dragged by the crew, over the narrow isthmus from Tarbert to the Atlantic, so making Kintyre an island of Norway. Bute was more easily defined.

The twelfth century appears to have brought varied fortunes. Celt and Viking mingled in the family of Somerled, the ancestors of the Lords of the Isles. Somerled, having conquered Bute, sailed across to Renfrew in 1164, with the unachieved aim of subduing Scotland. It is probable that Walter FitzAlan, Steward of Scotland, received Bute from Malcolm IV around this time. Certainly Rothesay Castle was under the command of the Steward of Scotland in 1228, when, according to the *Anecdotes of Olave the Black*, the Norwegians 'went to Bute, and the Scots lay there in a castle. They set down before the fortress, and gave a hard assault. The Scotch fought well, and threw upon them burning pitch and lead. They prepared over themselves a covering of boards, and then hewed down the walls, for the stone was soft, and the ramparts fell with them, and they cut it up from the foundation'.

The Norse chronicle records that King Haco had made Husbec feudatory king of the western isles, and provided him with arms to take possession of these dominions. On arriving off the coast of Scotland, Husbec was joined by Olave, King of the Isle of Man, which was then under Norse suzerainty. They collected troops from the islands under Norwegian influence

58

and sailed in eighty ships round the Mull of Kintyre to Bute, and made their attack on the Castle. Their hard-fought victory cost them 300 men, and Husbec himself was reported to have died of injuries received at the siege. The exact date of this changeover is uncertain, but the Castle was held by the Scots in 1228 and by the Vikings in 1230. Indeed, after 1230 the islands seemed to have become a permanent colony of Norway, or so King Haco thought. Alexander II unsuccessfully demanded they return to Scottish rule. His son, Alexander III, prepared to carry out his father's vow 'to plant the Scots Lion on Haco's furthest isle', and news of the preparations towards this end reached Bergen, where Haco held a council of war in the summer of 1263, then prepared for battle with characteristic Viking flamboyance. The great ships were ready—Haco's own man-of-war was 'constructed entirely of oak, and contained twenty-seven banks of oars. It was ornamented with heads and necks of dragons, beautifully overlaid with gold'. Haco boasted that he would 'sit upon the stern of his snorting steed adorned with ruddy gold'. The armada sailed from Herlover like the flight of 'sky-blue doves with their expanded wings'. The image of the wings over the sea seems real enough, although a Scottish witness would scarcely think of doves as the great fleet of 160 ships approached his shore.

Paradoxically these Vikings, like a later armada, were destroyed by the sea that had borne them so triumphantly over the summer months, when the seemingly tranquil waters of the Clyde changed before the full force of an Atlantic gale sweeping past Arran and the Cumbraes. Haco's depleted fleet found some shelter in the anchorage of Rothesay Bay before facing the decisive battle at Largs. This was the turning point for the Norsemen, and the next day they buried their dead. Haco waited around for two more days, and at the end of the week, accompanied by Magnus and the Somerled princes, set sail and anchored in the bay of Lamlash. 'The king then ordered the body of Ivar Holm' (one of his captains) 'to be carried to Bute

59

where it was interred.' The funeral galleon returned to the retreating fleet, and Haco died two months later in Orkney. Under his successor, Magnus IV, peace negotiations began, paving the way for the ceding of all the islands except Orkney and Shetland to Scotland. Thereafter, Bute and, indeed, most of Scotland, saw no more of the fierce Northern raiders.

THE STRUGGLE FOR INDEPENDENCE

Alexander the Steward had been in possession of the Castle when Haco was driven back at Largs, and his sons Alexander and John were great patriots at the time of Edward I. In 1286 they were with Bruce at Turnberry Castle, signing the 'Turnberry Bond' for mutual defence.

Until this time Rothesay had been the only Scottish castle without an English warden, but in 1292 John Baliol included Bute in the Sheriffdom of Kintyre, and again in 1296 the sons of Alexander swore fealty to Edward. This may have been a temporary and strategic defection, according to the practical politics of the time, when submission could be renewed without any change of heart. In any case they joined in Wallace's unsuccessful rebellion a year later. During the period of Wallace's defiance of the English, prominent Scottish loyalists, including the Bishop of Dunkeld, used Bute as a place of sanctuary while planning further measures against Edward, and, indeed, at this time Bute had become a rendezvous for leaders of the Scottish struggle for independence. The Steward of Rothesay Castle played a leading part with Wallace at Stirling Bridge, and at Falkirk, where Sir John Stewart led the Brandanes of Bute and died in the battle. His gravestone was a simple slab, marked in the old plan of Falkirk churchyard simply 'Stewart of Bute', but in 1877 the Marquess of Bute added a memorial cross with the inscription: 'In memory of the son of Bute, who, under Sir John Stuart, on the 22nd July 1298, in the battle near the Fawekirk, fought bravely and fell gloriously, this cross

60

is reverently raised by John Stuart, Marquess of Bute, A.D. 1877'.

After this act of commitment there was no way out for the Stewarts of the Castle. As punishment for the rebellion, Edward forfeited their lands and gave them to Alexander de Lindsay. The men of Bute continued to help Wallace in his unequal fight against the power of Edward. The execution of Wallace imposed a certain terror on the Scottish lords, and in 1305 James the Steward once again made his submission to Edward. However, when Robert Bruce had himself crowned as Scottish king at Scone in 1306, James acknowledged him as the rightful sovereign of Scotland.

Bute continued to be closely interested and involved in the struggle for independence. At the start of Robert Bruce's campaign Rothesay Castle was under the control of the English, but after the rebel Scots had taken Brodick Castle in Arran, the English left Bute. Walter, the son of James the Steward, took a prominent part in the battle of Bannockburn, and is mentioned in Barbour's *Brus*.

After the victory at Bannockburn Walter Stewart married Marjory Bruce, the daughter of Scotland's new king. Marjory died at the birth of her son Robert in 1316, and the baby was declared heir presumptive to the Scottish throne, after the king's son, David. Walter died in battle in 1326, and young Robert the Steward was actively engaged in the ensuing renewal of the war of independence. Fordun reports that 'He was a comely youth, tall and robust, modest, liberal, gay and courteous; and for innate sweetness of his disposition, generally beloved by true-hearted Scotsmen'. He was forced to take flight when Edward Baliol, assisted by the English, retook Rothesay Castle in 1334, and, although hunted throughout the island, managed with the help of local followers to escape to Dumbarton. Later he organised a revolt on the mainland, and took Dunoon Castle. When news of this success reached Bute, it roused great enthusiasm, and inspired the Brandanes to attack Rothesay Castle. The unarmed and unorganised crowd were driven back by the English garrison, but, after retreating up the slopes of Barone Hill, they found a rallying point in the old fort on the summit, and in a final act of defiance rushed down the hill, pelting the enemy with stones from the ancient building, breaking their ranks and capturing their weapons. They managed not only to win the encounter, but killed the Castle's English governor, Sir Adam Lisle.

The remarkable victory of Barone Hill proved a short-lived triumph, bringing swift retribution from Edward, who, in revenge for the killing of his governor, laid waste the island and reimposed English control on the castle.

After David had submitted to Edward in 1363 there was an attempt to impose a future English succession on Scotland, by acknowledging an English prince as heir to the Scottish throne in exchange for a treaty of perpetual peace. But this plan was successfully resisted by the Scottish Estates, who indignantly refused to sanction such an agreement, and declared that 'they would never permit an Englishman to reign over them'; they also confirmed the right of Robert the Steward to succeed to the Crown. He openly rebelled against England. He and his son were imprisoned in Loch Leven Castle, but when David died in 1371, he succeeded to the throne.

THE STEWARTS

Robert II, the first of the house of Stewart, was a frequent visitor to Rothesay Castle, where he died in 1390. During his reign a chapel was built within the castle walls, the defences were reorganised, and the curtain walls strengthened. Robert married twice, once to a distant relative, which necessitated his obtaining dispensation from the Pope to legitimise his children. His family was large, his son Robert succeeding him as Robert III, and his son John becoming Sheriff of the royal castle at Rothesay. The new king used the castle as a royal residence. His father in his old age had delighted to stay there, and the *Exchequer Rolls* of 1376 gives us an idea of the provisioning of the Castle when royalty was in residence. 'Pipes of wine, fat cattle, and other delicacies came for the use of the king— almost year after year—lampreys from the Forth, honey from Blackness, and from Linlithgow many a jar of red Rhine wine to swill down the huntsman's venison.' (The king had game-lands at Ormidale.) Robert III, although an unhappy man, in bad health, and an unfortunate ruler, made two notable decrees: the first in 1398 created his eldest son Duke of Rothesay, a title still bestowed on the heir apparent to the throne; and the second in 1401 granted a charter to the burgh of Rothesay.

The first decree brought little immediate advantage, and the first Duke of Rothesay did not live long to enjoy the honour. Robert left his affairs too much to his younger brother, the Duke of Albany, who carried on a bitter feud with his nephew, a feud that did little good to the Scottish cause. When the first Duke of Rothesay died in mysterious circumstances while confined in a dungeon, the general opinion was that Albany was the murderer, a view obviously shared by the king, who, fearing for his younger son, sent him to France—another unfortunate decision, since this son was captured at sea by the English.

The second decree, the granting of the charter, has a special interest, and the late Professor George Pryde, a distinguished Scottish historian, has pointed out that this charter is noteworthy as the first occasion in which the term 'royal burgh' is used in a Scottish document. Incidentally the burgh of Rothesay still has its original charters, although the council records for the first 250 years have been lost (or possibly, in the opinion of local historian Blain, carried away by Cromwell's Governor of the Castle at the time of the Civil War).

Robert III died in 1406, possibly, as some claim, in Rothesay Castle, or at Dundonald, and he is buried in Paisley Abbey. On his death the family of the Stewarts of Bute became keepers of Rothesay Castle, a right of residence that was confirmed as a hereditary title in 1498, when James IV granted the keeping of the Castle to Ninian Stewart. This title has continued until the present day, with the Marquess of Bute still recognised as Keeper of the Castle. During the troubled times of James II there was rebellion under the Lord of the Isles. The Castle of Rothesay held, and in 1458, two years before his death, the king came to Rothesay.

In the reign of James III the Crown lands in Bute were given to a kinsman, who became Earl of Arran, but James IV granted the stewartry in Bute to Hugh, Lord Montgomery, and after making Ninian Stewart hereditary keeper, he later in 1506 granted charters of the lands to his tenants in Bute. Thus most of the landholders on the island obtained their feu-charters from the king.

Before the accession of the Steward's family to the throne, the Stewart lands had been the proper inheritance of the family. The value of these lands in Bute, Cumbrae, Cowal and Kintyre was £1,000 Scots in 1366, when the eldest son of the king had a life rent of the Crown lands. From 1469 the charters were sealed by the eldest son as 'Prince and Steward of Scotland', and in November of that year an act was passed declaring that the lands belonged to the first-born prince of the royal house.

James IV in the course of his voyages in his warship to subdue the rebellious Highlanders of Kintyre, made visits to Rothesay Castle in 1494, and in subsequent years held courts in Bute. Rothesay was the scene of many court assemblies around the turn of the century, and the Castle was again regarded as a royal residence.

During the reigns of James IV and James V Rothesay Castle became important as a base of operations against the rebellious Scots, and the frequent visits of both monarchs was partly due to this factor. The Castle was improved considerably during this period. In 1512 James IV began the construction of the great dungeon tower, a work that was finally completed by his son James V in 1512.

Troubled times recurred during the regency period when

James V was still young. In 1527 the Master of Ruthven and five associates obtained remission for treason in laying siege to Rothesay Castle and burning the 'town of Bute'. It appears from old records that the royal burgh of Rothesay had been reduced to ashes during the attack, but that the strong castle had held out successfully. There were constant hereditary feudings around the castles of Bute, Arran and Argyll, and sometimes the men of Bute were not on the defence. In 1528 the sons of Ninian Stewart attacked Brodick Castle, property of the Hamiltons, and James Stewart, Sheriff of Bute, afterwards took over the estates; but in 1549 he was compelled to yield up the Arran lands. There were regular raids, too, between the Campbells of Argyll and their neighbours.

One of the first visits of James V to Bute followed his abortive voyage to France in 1536, his companion on this occasion being Sir James Hamilton, who was later executed as a traitor, one of the accusations being that, having obtained 3,000 crowns from the king to repair and appoint Rothesay Castle as a royal residence, he had failed to perform the work and account for the money.

Four years later, in the summer of 1540, the king made a naval expedition round Scotland with twelve ships, to impress the western clans and attack the pirates who were harrying the shipping routes. On his return he visited Bute, and in the following year gave orders for the completion of the castle improvements, including the great barbican tower.

After James V's death in 1542, Scotland was once again a regency, and the Earl of Lennox intrigued with the English, invading Bute in 1544, and putting it to fire and sword. An interesting record of this episode is found in the sixteenth-century calendar of state papers of Scotland, stating, 'May 1544 —Instruction to Sir Richard Mansel and Richbroke to take possession of the castle of Rosse and the Isle of Bute on behalf of the king.' A further extract records: 'June 26—Agreement between Henry VIII and the Earl of Lennox whereby the earl agrees to surrender to the king the castles of Dumbarton and Isle of Bute'.

In 1588 a proclamation by James VI was read at the Cross in Rothesay High Street, calling the men to arms against the Armada. The muster saw no action, as the Armada was wrecked by storms, one ship being sunk off Portincross. In 1598 there was a muster of men against the islesmen.

Towards the end of the sixteenth century, Bute, despite its long historical record, was still in many respects an almost unknown island. George Buchanan's *History of Scotland*, written in 1582, refers to the Island of 'Boot'—'It hath but one town in it, bearing the name of the Island; and in it an old Castle called Rothesay'. Nevertheless early documents exist, with records of fair days like St Blane's on 12 August, and details of cattle swimming across the Narrows, or being ferried to Kerrycroy for such occasions. Apart from the historical documents, interesting relics of the medieval period have been discovered. Longhouses excavated at Little Dunagoil in 1960 yielded glazed pottery of the thirteenth century and a corn-drying kiln. Parts of medieval buildings are still to be found, including the square fourteenth-century tower of Kames Castle, Ascog House, and the Mansion House in Rothesay's High Street. Crowners Castle is a good example of one of the sixteenth-century residences of the landowners of the time who held great power, administering justice on their own land, and having the authority to order hanging for crimes like sheep-stealing.

AFTER THE UNION

In the main the Stewarts of Bute were loyalists. At the time of the Battle of Langside James Stewart supported Mary, and fought for her. Bute on the whole supported the Covenant. Hector Bannatyne of Kames signed as representative of the landowners of Bute, and Matthew Spence for the burgesses of Rothesay.

During the reign of Charles I, Lamont of Toward and Ascog Castles remained a royalist and fought for the king against Argyll. The High Steward of the Castle was ruined by his loyalty to the king. The Sheriff, another of the name of James Stewart, garrisoned Rothesay Castle with his own vassals. After the royal army under Montrose had defeated the Campbells at Inverlochy, the Sheriff was placed in command of two armed frigates in an attempt to capture Dumbarton Castle, but the enterprise failed and he had to escape to Ireland. Ultimately he was required to pay a fine of 5,000 marks to regain his office and property.

The Campbells took their revenge on those who had supported the king, the episode being the ground for one of the indictments that brought Archibald, Marquess of Argyll, to the block for high treason 15 years later. What happened was that Sir James Lamont, who had fought against Argyll, had retired to his castles at Toward and Ascog, but in 1646 the Campbells destroyed them both, murdered the occupants, including serving women and young children. Sir James was imprisoned and misused at Inverary, but the other captives were taken to the Castle of Dunoon and hanged. There is a formidable list of the executed, including the provost and several townsmen of Rothesay. Argyll's defence was that he had a royal commission to punish Lamont, but that did not save him from being beheaded for this and other acts of treason in 1661.

With the success of Cromwell, a standing army under General Monk kept the country in peace. An English garrison held the Castle of Rothesay; Cromwell's men laid the defences waste and fired the castle before withdrawing in 1659. There was no covenanting in Bute, and the island declared its support for Charles II.

When James VII (James II of England) came to the throne in 1685, the Highland insurgents seized Bute for a time, and when William and Mary were proclaimed king and queen, the Bute militia were called out in anticipation of possible Jacobite

67

intrigues. During the 1685 rebellion, the followers of the Duke of Argyll overran Bute, plundered the town of Rothesay, and burned the Castle, after which it remained ruined and uninhabitable. The Bute family, who had lived in the Castle for 200 years as stewards, moved to the Mansion House in the High Street. This building has now been restored and is used as the Bute Estate Office.

The Sheriff of Bute was appointed Commissioner to the Union of Parliaments, and in 1703 was raised to the peerage as the Earl of Bute. This was the first occasion on which the Stewarts held the title, which has been retained until the present. The Bute family has remained prominent in national and local government affairs. The third Earl (1713–92) was tutor to George III, and later became Secretary of State and George III's first Prime Minister, wielding a strong influence on policy.

Bute is fortunate in having a collection of local records that help to tell something of the social history of the seventeenth, eighteenth, and nineteenth centuries. Reports of court cases range from capital offences to the most trivial (although the punishments did not always recognise this distinction). In 1673 a trial for witchcraft led to the last execution for this crime taking place at the traditional Gallows Craig, at the foot of Rothesay's Gallowgate. In the same year it was also recorded that 'Mary Campbell is ordered to leave the parish because she sometimes reads cups for amusement'.

There is an order in existence, dated 1679, from the Earl of Argyll to the Laird of Kames for the militia to be ready to deal with Popish rebels and outlaws in the Highlands. Ten days after the arrival of the Prince of Orange in England in November 1688 it is recorded that 'Sir James Stewart is empowered by the Privy Council to convene and keep together in arms for His Majesty's service, and defence of the shire of Bute, the militia force, and do everything else that might best conduce to His Majesty's service and the peace of the shire.'

On a lighter note the clock and bell of Rothesay's Tolbooth

received serious attention in the burgh proceedings of that time. A new bell was ordered in 1686, to be rung 'dayly in the morning at six o'clock betwixt Michelmas and Patrickmes and after Patrickmes till Michelmas at five o'cloack and dayly during the year at eight of cloak at night'. A year later, apparently as an afterthought, a new belfry was ordered 'for carrying the new common bell of the Burgh soe that the same may be useful to the haill inhabitants yrof, so that they may hear not only the same rung, butt also the cloak strykeing yron', and an accompanying item in the Burgh accounts lists a charge 'for oyle at the dighting of the knock'. An interesting item in the Council records reports that 'the last of the expeditions under the Darien scheme sailed from Rothesay Bay on the 14th September 1699, consisting of four frigates with 1200 emigrants'.

During the rebellion of 1715, the second Earl of Bute was Lord Lieutenant of Buteshire, and 'commanded the Militia and fencible men of that shire and of Argyll at Inveraray, and preserved the quiet of the country'.

In 1764 the Earl of Bute began a campaign to improve and develop natural resources on the island, and in 1765 Rothesay became a Customs House Station, and later a licensed herring fishery. In the following quarter of a century the fishing industry was extended, the new cotton industry started, and many agricultural improvements introduced. Road repairs were undertaken, and a regular ferry service established from Kilmichael. An indication of the general expansion was provided by the increase of population from 2,600 to 4,800 during this period.

Increasing social responsibility is indicated in items bearing the same date in 1795—'Council contributes fifteen guineas towards the expense of procuring an engine for extinguishing fires, in conjunction with the cotton works', and 'Council agrees to apply to the trustees of the Cumbray lighthouse, as they have a superfluity of funds, that they may erect a lighthouse on Toward Point.' Two handwritten documents of the early nineteenth century have been preserved in the Bute Natural History Society library, the first being a list of 'householders on whom notices have been served respecting militiamen', and the second, a roll of the parish of Rothesay in 1815, showing many present-day family and street names, the latter including High Street, Watergate Street, Montague Street, and Mill Lade. *Fowler's Commercial Directory* for 1834 notes that Rothesay possesses 'excellent inns, coffee houses, and a flourishing harbour and herring trade'. The steam packets to Glasgow are listed, and reference made to the Bute Arms Coffee Rooms, first opened in 1790, and later frequented by Edmund Kean on his visits to Bute.

In 1833 at the first election after the Reform Act, the Marquess of Bute was again elected Provost of Rothesay, and in the following year instigated street-widening improvements, recommended the lighting of the town with gas, granted a piece of ground from his estates to increase the burying ground, and presented a clock for the new town hall.

By mid-century Rothesay was a thriving town with a richly varied life of its own. The citizens, who had been disturbed in 1813 by the sight of Henry Bell's *Comet* steaming in Rothesay Bay, soon adapted themselves to the new means of communication, and the harbour became a scene of continuous activity. The older industries were now supplemented by an emerging tourist trade, but even as late as 1872 over 600 still worked at the two main spinning and weaving mills. In that year the Esplanade was completed as an attraction for the greatly increasing number of holidaymakers. A Physical and Archaeological Society was founded by five young men of the town, and a lecture was given by the Marquess of Bute. A museum was started, and the first aquarium in Scotland was opened. Bute, though obviously on the threshold of an era of change, was reasonably confident of its ability to maintain its position.

Page 71   (above) Kerrycroy
Village: this model village
was designed by the first
Marquess, with later additions
by successors; (below) auto-
matic sluice at Kirk Dam: the
water power for the mills was
doubled by Thom's pioneering
enterprise in diverting, direct-
ing, and storing the island's
supply

Page 72 (above) Woodend House (Kean's cottage): this beautiful house on the shores of Loch Fad, was built for famous actor Edmund Kean, whose link with Bute spanned the last ten years of his life; (below) another view of Kerrycroy, the model village planned by members of the Bute family

THE TWENTIETH CENTURY

The high-water mark of Rothesay as a holiday resort, and the Firth of Clyde as a sailing centre, was reached in the last quarter of the nineteenth century and the years before World War I. But apart from her new role as tourist centre, Bute's life had taken on a different pattern at the beginning of the twentieth century. The great days of the cotton mills and the fishing fleets had passed, and other aspects had changed also. Up till the last years of the nineteenth century Gaelic had been spoken, particularly in north Bute, but from then on there was a rapid decline in the use of the language, and by the 1950s there were less than fifty islanders who could speak it at all. Communities that had been self-supporting began to decline—places like Straad and Kerrycroy, and even the larger Kilchattan Bay, lost their occupations. Their harbours declined and the centre of activity moved even more definitely to Rothesay.

Newspaper cuttings in the last years before World War I gave evidence of local activities ranging from renewed efforts to find workable coal seams on the island to preparations for the visit to Rothesay of Sir J. Forbes Robertson in *Hamlet*. Surprisingly the war had no spectacular effect on Bute, although the rapid development of the petrol engine, and the consequent appearance of motor vehicles and motorboats, made for important long-term changes.

Between the wars Rothesay's role seemed to move further towards concentration on tourism, and despite a gradual decline in steamer sailings, Bute maintained its position as a premier holiday resort. In 1936 new swimming baths were opened, and in 1937 the new Rothesay Pavilion, which served as dance-hall, concert-hall, restaurant, and conference centre, was built.

World War II affected the people of Bute much more than its predecessor. The island had a large influx of evacuees, the exiled Polish Army found a long-term base in Rothesay, and a

E

Commando training area was established at Inchmarnock, which was taken over completely for the purpose. Most important was the use of Rothesay as a naval centre for nearly the whole of the war, and for many years after its conclusion. Rothesay Bay was the base for the third submarine squadron, with the *Cyclops*, and later the *Montclare*, acting as depot ships for the flotilla of operational submarines until the final closure in 1957.

Port Bannatyne was used as the base for the Liverpool & Glasgow Salvage Company, and provided the location for the final scenes of some epic wartime sagas. Local newspaper editor John Mackenzie, who had a journalistic career spanning nearly 70 years, recounts several stories in his book *Country Editor*. When one of the children's evacuee ships, *Volendam*, was torpedoed on a transatlantic voyage, she managed to stay afloat, and was able to return to Port Bannatyne, where she was beached for repairs. An examination revealed an unexploded torpedo which, had it exploded with the other, must have sunk the ship. The function of this yard at 'the Port' was to give first aid to those ships sufficiently seaworthy to continue up river for further service in the yards, or alternatively to break up the vessels that were beyond salvage. Many a grim scene occurred when victims of below-deck explosions had to be extricated from twisted wreckage, sometimes for mass burial at local churchyards.

Perhaps the most notable visitor to the bay was that famous survivor of the *Jervis Bay* convoy, the burned and shelled tanker *San Demetrio*. Mr Mackenzie writes of his assignment as the first correspondent to interview the crew, and retell the story of how they took to the lifeboats when their ship caught fire, then, noticing that the fire was dying down, decided to reboard the ship, and managed to put out the flames. The bridge, with its charts and compasses, had been destroyed, and all these sixteen men had was a school atlas to navigate by. They managed to restart the engines, however, and finally sighted land off

County Mayo, where they were met by a naval tug offering a tow. This they refused, but gladly accepted a store of provisions, and the help of volunteers from the destroyer *Arrow*. They made their way up the Firth of Clyde into Rothesay Bay with a huge SOS painted on the burnt bridge, and anchored safely after their epic voyage.

Another casualty of the war at sea was the tanker *Imperial Transport*, and this amazing episode, later headlined nationally as the 'voyage of half-a-ship', also ended in Bute. Again Mr Mackenzie recounted the story in *Country Editor*:

> The tanker was split in half by a torpedo. The crew got into the lifeboats, but when they found the stern half still floating, reboarded it, got the engine started, and brought her into the Clyde, an amazing feat of seamanship. She was beached at Kilchattan Bay, and lay there for over a year, while a new bow section was built upriver. Officers of the ship lived ashore in Bute while the ship was beached, and made many friends.

Rothesay was very much a naval town at that time. Apart from the battle-scarred torpedoed ships in the bays, the crews of the submarines and depot ship were ferried back and forward in the liberty boats, and made their presence felt in various ways. As always there was a lighter side to balance the grim stories. On one occasion the Rothesay town councillors were invited for a voyage on a submarine, and as they left the the bay were given the opportunity to experience a period of submersion. A resident who had been watching at Ardencraig telephoned the police that the submarine had sunk off Ascog. Apparently rumours spread and there was some alarm in the town. In due course the councillors arrived back, to be welcomed with some relief by the apprehensive, while the more cynical citizens questioned if the safe return of the Town Council was a matter for congratulation or regret.

The cynics also indulged themselves at the expense of the depot ships *Cyclops* and *Montclare*, whose servicing duties allowed them to leave their anchorage only for short spells every six months. Opinion was divided as to whether the reason for these periodic departures was to allow the crew to qualify for duty-free spirits and cigarettes, or to provide an opportunity for clearing the mound of jettisoned tin cans that the ship was alleged to be sitting on!

Rothesay presented a strange and sometimes striking picture in those years. At times the old dream of a Firth of Clyde teeming with seagoing traffic, and a bay alive with ships, be-came a reality once again, although in a more sombre setting, with grey camouflaged warships substituting for the colour of earlier days. Yet it was still a bravely impressive sight when a long convoy of warships and merchantmen, and mighty liners like *Queen Mary* or *Queen Elizabeth* acting as troop-carriers, sailed past the point, while others lay quietly at their moorings in the bay.

After the war, and particularly following the final departure of the submarine depot ship in 1957, Rothesay returned to its former role of the commercial and marketing centre for the island's 7,000 residents, and the focal point for another 20,000 holiday visitors. For a time at least her history rests there, with the main events chronicled relating to past rather than present. Since then a grand pageant in 1951 has celebrated the 550th anniversary of the granting of Rothesay's charter; the Castle's restored Great Hall was reopened in 1970; and there was the visit of another Duke of Rothesay (Prince Charles) to revive memories of an ancient title and royal link.

5   AGRICULTURE, FISHING, & INDUSTRY

THE main industry of Bute from the days of its earliest inhabitants has been farming. At the present time agriculture is possibly more dominant than ever, as the once thriving fishing industry is in decline, and outside the parish of Rothesay work on the land provides practically the sole occupation.

In north Bute there are forty-five farm steadings (including two on the island of Inchmarnock), most of them at least a century old, with over 6,000 acres in crops and grass. Dairy farming, mainly with Ayrshire cattle, is predominant, and fifty of the eighty-four full-time farms are dairy farms.

Kingarth parish has twenty-six arable farms, twelve small holdings, and two sheep farms. Here again dairy farming, featuring such famous pedigree herds as Mid Ascog, Bruchag, Meikle Kilmory, and Kerrytonlia, is supreme. In addition to these and other well known prize-winning Ayrshire breeds, the Marquess of Bute keeps a herd of Highland cattle at the Plan farm. Beef cattle also have some importance, and their numbers are increasing.

Great attention is given to the quality of the dairy cattle, all the herds in the parish being tuberculin-tested, and it has been reported recently that Bute is one of the few areas in Scotland to be declared completely free of brucellosis.

Early potatoes are a feature of the sheltered and sandy-soiled southern corner, over 150 acres being given over to preparing this important crop for the Glasgow market. Epicures from

Dunagoil farm have on occasion been on sale as early as the first days of June, and are regularly ready before the middle of the month. The peak of this specialisation was probably during the 1890s and 1900s, but there is still a thriving market for Bute's delightfully flavoured 'new potatoes'.

The parish of Rothesay contains fourteen farms, all dairy, and the pattern is similar in the rest of the island, although the proximity of the main population centre affects marketing. Agriculture is obviously a thriving industry on the island at present, and the trend of development towards the present position makes an interesting study.

The celebrated find of that grain of wheat in the Neolithic domestic site at Townhead belongs to archaeology rather than history, but it indicates that around 2500 BC the earliest primitive farming existed in Bute. The varied selection of querns discovered during successive excavations indicates developments in the methods used for grinding the corn grown by these first farmers. The earliest method was by pounding in a mortar, a technique still used alongside more advanced ones in first century Roman times. Rubbing stones led to saddle querns, which in turn were replaced by rotary mills around 100 BC.

The early Christian missionaries farmed around St Blane's, where remains of a corn-drying kiln may be seen, while the Vikings, though more notable for their sailing and raiding exploits, were also good farmers, and left traces of their agricultural activities on the island.

By the fourteenth century a primitive but roughly planned pattern had developed. A little bread was made from grain, the daily porridge provided, some dairy cattle kept, and a crude form of butter, curd, and cheese making was undertaken. During the reigns of Robert II and Robert III, when the kings stayed for considerable periods at the royal castle of Rothesay, reference to farming is found in the records. The *Exchequer Rolls* of 1376 and subsequent years include items like 'fat cattle for the use of the king'.

During the following century the various farm lands are beginning to be defined. The *Exchequer Rolls* for 1450 give the names of tenants in Bute, including 'the Makkaws of Garrochty, the Makwerdys, Bannachtyne, Makalesters, Stewarts, Jamie-sons', among them farmers whose descendants play a prominent part in modern Bute agriculture.

In 1474 it was recorded that James Stewart, Sheriff of Bute, obtained from James III a grant of an acre of land in Kilchattan, with liberty to erect a mill. The remains of the steading are still visible on this site. The King's Mill in Rothesay was built in 1480 and continued to grind corn for over 450 years until it was destroyed by fire during World War II. It stood on the Lade in John Street. To it all the lands in Bute were 'thirled' or attached for obtaining their milling. In 1491 a mill was built on the Kames lands, long held by the famous North Bute family of Bannatyne.

In 1506 James IV granted charters of the lands of his tenants in Bute to be held on the payment of fixed fermes and the giving of service. So most of the landholders on the island got their feu-charters direct from the king. In return each tenant was bound to furnish a mart to the royal table for every 5 marks of rent payable by him, for which mart he received the sum of 5s from the chamberlain. These marts had to be transported to the mainland for distribution to the various castles where the court assembled. For this purpose the ferry from Kerrycroy to Portincross on the Ayrshire mainland was used, and another boat plied between Bute and Cowal, the ferryman receiving annually a boll of barley out of the rents.

As early as the seventeenth century definite measures were being taken to improve farming on the island. On 14 March 1678 it was 'enacted, for the promoting of agriculture and improvement of land that every person in the royalty occupying land soe half a fourth part of peas in proportion to every boll sowing of oats or bear he has, under penalty of forty shillings'. 'Enacted also, that it shall not be lawful for any person to keep

79

bee-skapes within the town, except those who are worth a yearly free rent of £10 besides his dwelling-house and yard, or such as pay £10 of rent to another within the same.' Although those not authorised to keep skapes, were told to remove them quickly, under penalty of a fine and confiscation, the clerk and doctor were excepted, and licensed to keep one skape each, even if they were not 'heritors or renters of land'.

The second and third Earls of Bute were pioneering enthusiasts in new agricultural methods. They offered subsidies and premiums for development, encouraged attendance at agricultural courses, including a farmer's training course at Melrose in the Borders, and made many contributions towards improvement. Blain in his history describes many of the earls' efforts to help farming, and refers to such developments as harrowing with iron pins, the herding of cattle, and the provision of a cattle ferry. John Blain himself experimented with the use of coraline, gathered at St Ninian's cockle shore, in order to sweeten the rather acid soil. That predated the liming of fields, with limekilns in use at Scalpsie. Steps were also taken to assess farms, an example being at Kilmichael in 1790.

The third Earl's expert interest in botany encouraged him to continue his father's work in developing the splendid collection of trees in Mount Stuart grounds. In 1737 he started a 'Journall of the Planting etc. executed at Mountstewart from the first laying out of the Gardens', which was kept for many years, together with the head gardener's daily record of work and weather.

His successors continued to improve and experiment in agriculture. The fourth Earl who became first Marquess, furthered this policy by employing two agricultural experts in 1804 to report on conditions on his tenants' farms, and advise on improvements. Seven years later 'Mr. Adam Walker of Mellandean, Roxburghshire, the first farmer in the South of Scotland' was asked to make observations on the state of agriculture in Bute, and there was a subsequent exchange of young Bute and Roxburgh farmworkers.

The second Marquess followed his grandfather's agricultural policy, and the Bute *Record of Rural Affairs*, published in 1839, refers to experiments in self-feed silage during the years 1810–35. During these and subsequent years the Butes continued systematically to acquire nearly all the farms on the island, establishing a pattern that remains a unique modern relic of benevolent feudalism.

Obviously the island's agricultural policy has been and is affected by the strong controlling interest of the Marquess of Bute, who now owns 95 per cent of the eighty-four farms. Eight of these are administered by the Bute Estate Office and the remainder rented on a landlord-tenant basis. There are also six part-time farm units, and a number of spare-time small-holdings. These farms are mostly of a handy manageable size, averaging 136 acres of arable land and 22 acres of pasture. The tenant-farmers are enterprising and advanced in most respects, and in part at least this results from the assurance given by the enlightened policy of recent and present land-owners, which offers security together with encouragement towards improvement. The Bute Estate manages several farms directly, and maintains a keen interest in the welfare of the others. In the view of those most closely concerned it would be difficult to fault the general results of this agricultural policy. In some ways the system has allowed a better than average deal for both farmer and worker. A larger proportion of men working on Bute farms become tenants in their own right than any-where on the mainland. It is important and relevant to note that one-third of the farms let in recent years have been allotted to working men from other farms. The farms and farm build-ings, the well kept attractive houses, the freshly painted white steadings, the trim farmyards, neat hedges, and well worked fields are features of the Bute landscape, and the farms of the island must rank very high in appearance and efficiency.

Before 1914, farming on Bute, as in most of Scotland, provided a poor and chancy living, but the situation has improved greatly during the past few decades, which have seen a period of increasing mechanisation, intensive cultivation, and steady progress towards greater productivity. The emerging specialisation on dairy farming has proved mainly successful, making for quality as well as quantity. The growing prominence of Bute pedigree stock is noteworthy, but of equal importance is the island's claim to be one of the first areas in Scotland to be wholly attested and brucellosis-free. The present daily yield of milk is well over 4,000 gallons in summer, and perhaps half that in winter. The creamery in Rothesay, as well as pasteurising, bottling, and distributing the milk, manufactures over 200 tons of cheese annually.

Linked with the growing strength of dairy farming and an increase in the number of beef cattle, Bute has now nearly 12,000 acres in crops and grass. Oats was for many years the dominant crop; there was little wheat, and up till fairly recently little barley, but much more is grown now, and it is rapidly becoming the main crop. Turnips and kale are grown extensively to supplement winter feeding, while haystacks have been mostly replaced by silage pits and towers.

The sheep population has doubled since 1939, and one of Bute's best known and greatly admired local historians calculated that in 1954 there were 11,000 sheep in the parishes of north Bute and Kingarth, and one in the parish of Rothesay, adding dryly that he suspected the one in Rothesay to be 'an elderly ewe of character and distinction'. The sheep, mainly blackface, continue to increase in numbers, and in addition several thousand ewes cross from Argyll by Rhubodach ferry to winter on the island.

Poultry are estimated to total over 20,000, mostly regarded as a small-scale farming sideline, although there are now three large-scale certificated poultry farms on the island.

In the ploughing world the striking postwar feature has been mechanisation, with the triumph of the tractor and the disappearance of the working horse. In 1857 there were 667 working horses on the island; in 1906, 180 selected Clydesdales —the pick of several hundreds—were sent to Ayr show, and even as late as 1954 there were 259 horses on the island. Since then the decline has been continuous and rapid, and there must now be few if any horses on Bute.

Mechanisation has also led to a decline in the number of agricultural labourers, recorded as 326 in 1943, 291 in 1954, and 195 in 1955. The 1970 estimate was just over 150.

FISHING

Fishing rivals agriculture as the oldest human occupation, and one of the earliest industries. In ancient times the first dwellers in Bute caught fish by means of tidal fish-traps, and remains of these constructions have been found at eight points on the western shore and one on the east. This survey is not yet complete, but it is obvious that primitive fishing was widespread on the island. The use of fish-traps probably began in Mesolithic times, and did not completely die out in the Highlands and islands until very recently.

Bute's best preserved fish-trap is at Mechnock, while other interesting examples have been found at Glecknabae, St Ninian's, and Carrick Point. The principle behind the working and selective baiting of those early traps has not yet been discovered, and so far little is known beyond the obvious use of the tide. John Ferrier, in his interesting report in the 1969 *Transactions of the Buteshire Natural History Society*, speculates on the possible relation between the positioning of deserted crofting sites and fish-traps, pointing to the farming-fishing combination that was the true crofter's way of life over hundreds of years. The cave at Dunagoil provides evidence of the presence of fishermen among the various members of the early community.

Coming to more recent times it seems certain that fish were

much more plentiful around the shores 200 years ago. Before 1765, although fishing in Bute was chiefly carried on with boats of under 5 tons, and only a few from 10 to 20 tons, the extent of trade and profits was remarkable.

Local historian Blain, who was collector of Customs, confirms that from 1749 to 1757 the net profits rose from approximately £1,300 to £2,434. This success encouraged the building of larger boats, and in 1799, when the tonnage bounty came to be given by the government, sixty-eight vessels were fitted out by the Rothesay group, totalling 3,316 tons, and employing crews to the number of 781 men. They were very successful in that year, many of them securing two cargoes, so that they took and cured nearly 50,000 barrels of herring. An additional hazard of the time was indicated in the burgh record of 17 December 1794. 'Seven men engaged in herring fishing have been impressed into the navy. On representation that the fishermen were deserting their occupation six of them were released.'

In 1800 there were eighty-nine vessels, totalling 4,403 tons, and carrying 1,027 men. This success tempted many to try the Firth of Forth in addition to west-coast fishing, but over-ambition led to disastrous results in 1801. During the next few years there was varying success and slightly diminishing numbers, and Blain considered that, with the abolition of the royal bounty, 'the Rothesay fishing trade, although considerable, had not advanced so much as the apparent advantages of the harbour would lead one to expect'.

This harbour mentioned by Blain had a very long history. Back on 30 June 1665 a burgh minute noted that 'the whole inhabitants are obliged to contribute towards repairing the harbour'. A century later the Rothesay quay, which had been continuously maintained by the local inhabitants, had again fallen into decay, and in 1755 the Rothesay Council decided to rebuild it; with the aid of small grants and some voluntary help by the townsfolk a quay 200yd long, 30ft broad, with a harbour depth of 10–12ft was completed. In 1789 the harbour was improved by the addition of the west pier, and again in 1800 it was further extended. Once more the piers were repaired and rebuilt in 1822, when the whole plan was completed, the unique double harbour now enlarged and linked by a drawbridge.

The fishing industry in Bute reached its peak around the mid-nineteenth century. In 1837, fifty-eight vessels sailed from Rothesay, varying in size from 15 to 300 tons. A total of 255 men worked on them, and it was recorded that 90,000 barrels of salt herring were sent to market. This was the heyday of the great Firth of Clyde fishing fleet, and Rothesay provided a natural centre for the booming trade. In 1855 no fewer than 557 boats were registered in the town, with a working total of 1,654 fishermen. By 1864 the numbers employed had risen to 1,721, and although there were fewer boats (320) they were larger vessels, ranging from 15 to 280 tons. The two harbours, inner and outer, were very much larger than their present-day successors, and sheltered a great flotilla, which made the place seem alive with boats.

Those great shoals of herring in Loch Fyne have become legendary—the name itself became synonomous with fresh herring—and for over 100 years throughout the country, and as far afield as Germany and Russia, herring were bought for salting.

The special boat known as the Loch Fyne skiff was about 32ft long and 9ft broad, and deeper in the stern. The tanned brown lugsail and small jib on the bowsprit were characteristic features.

The Ardmaleish shipbuilding yard built most of the vessels, but there were other suppliers, including a Tarbert firm. The simple design and comparative cheapness of these boats allowed families to own one easily, and apart from Rothesay and neighbouring Port Bannatyne, every sheltered bay and natural harbour in the Firth had its little fishing community and small fleet of boats. In Victorian times each community had 'skiffs and gear, tall poles for drying and repairing nets, boilers for

85

tanning sails, pots for tarring ropes and handlines, forge and anvil for anchors, chains and ironwork, creels, lobster pots, boxes. . . .' Kilchattan Bay in its earliest days was an example of a thriving fishing village.

Boat design did not alter for a number of years, and the coming of the inboard engine in 1908 was the first fundamental change, with further developments in size and power following rapidly after that. The decline of the Loch Fyne herring industry, however, had started around the turn of the century. Catches became noticeably smaller and the yearly return of the shoals more erratic, and from that point there was a steady decrease in trade until by the mid-1920s only half a dozen herring boats remained at Rothesay. The 'mystery' of the disappearing Loch Fyne herring became a talking-point for Clydesiders for generations, and although the problem has never been fully solved, many experts blame the lack of a close season in the year-long sequence of indiscriminate netting.

An unexpected and fairly spectacular return of the herring took place in the late 1920s and early 1930s, when drifters and other vessels came from all over Scotland, and even Ireland, to share in the harvest. For a time the picturesque glories of the harbour alive with boats and the fisherwomen gutting the fish by the light of paraffin flares were partly restored.

A distinct lull followed this brief resurgence, and since the end of World War II a different pattern of fishing has emerged: the fishermen of Bute now concentrate in the main on white fish, with Rothesay the only commercial fishing centre on the island. It is now true to say that catches of white fish have completely replaced those of herring around the Clyde. In its own way development here has been impressive. The 1950 catch of under 10,000 stones had increased to over 80,000 stones by 1955, and now catches of cod, whiting, and haddock predominate, with a lesser amount of flatfish.

Rothesay's present-day fishing fleet, consisting of ten motor-drifters at the time of the third *Statistical Account* in the 1950s was further reduced by 1970, when only forty men were registered as employed in fishing. These boats, carrying a crew of five, are cruiser stern boats of approximately 20 tons; they range between 40 and 50ft in length, and are powered by Diesel engines. They are expensive vessels, furnished with very modern equipment.

Rothesay's fishing industry casts only an occasional backward look at those brave days of colour and excitement, when 500 boats could fill the bay with sail and the herring swam plentifully round the sea-lochs of the Clyde; for the successors of last century's fishermen of Bute are reasonably satisfied with a steady, if less spectacular, industry that is an important part of the island's economy.

COTTON

In the latter part of the eighteenth century and first half of the nineteenth Bute's cotton industry shared with agriculture and fishing the role of chief employers of labour. This prominence extended until at least 1860, and for a period of over 60 years up to 14 per cent of the population were employed in the cotton mills.

In the eighteenth century a small linen industry had developed in Rothesay, using flax grown locally, and operating by water-power on a lade running from Kirk Dam at the northern end of Loch Fad. Arkwright had received his spinning patent in 1769, and James Kenyon, who had connections with the inventor, arranged for some associates to set up a cotton mill in Rothesay in 1779. A factor in the choice of site was a readily available water supply.

Until fairly recently Rothesay's mill was listed as Scotland's first cotton mill, but it is now acknowledged that, although little came of the enterprise, a mill had been erected a year earlier in Penicuik, relegating Rothesay to second place. The confusion arose partly through the difficulty of keeping track of the tremendous expansion that took place in those early years. Henry Hamilton in his book *The Industrial Revolution in Scotland* states: 'The first mill was erected at Rothesay in 1779 and in the course of eight years nineteen mills including the famous New Lanark mills were erected'. Later in the book Hamilton writes: 'In 1779 the first effective cotton mill in Scotland was erected at Rothesay. The building was of two stories, measuring 42 feet by 13 feet and was said to have accommodation for 1000 spindles'.

Private papers preserved by the Marquess of Bute at Mount Stuart throw some light on priorities and early development. A letter dated 18 September 1777 was sent by Peter May, who had just been appointed factor to Lord Bute, to John Blain, Sheriff Clerk, Rothesay, who was always closely involved in Bute Estate affairs. Extracts indicate early moves towards setting up a mill in Rothesay:

> Nothing so far as I know has yet been done about the Lint Mill —I wish with all my heart that something could be done so as to establish a good Lint mill.—It will prevent any outcry if a Lint mile can be once set a-going, but the operator should be not only expert, but his integrity beyond suspicion.

In notes written earlier that summer Peter May stated:

> The situation of Bute is favourable for Trade and Commerce— severall attempts have already been made to establish and promote the Linen Manufacture in Bute, but a great deal yet remains—

while he observed around the same time:

> Manufactures are yet very little established on the Island and this is the more unaccountable considering its vicinity to Glasgow and Paisley, two of the greatest manufacturing Towns in Scotland. Glasgow in particular buys Linnen yearn from the remotest parts of the north and carries it overland. Why should Bute not avail itself of its contiguity to a large Trading Town of so much consequence to other places.

(*above*) Bute Looms: developing from a handcraft home industry to a large-scale power loom manufacturing company, they have made an impact on the fashion world, and provided a successful new industry for the island; (*below*) Rothesay Seafoods: Rothesay's newest industry is the development of the scallop market and it employs up to seventy, and has a number of local-based and more distant fishing boats under contract

Page 90 (above) Inland scene: south end of Bute; (below) the Sleeping Warrior: a view of Arran hills from south-west Bute, with one of the island's attractive farms in the foreground

In April 1778 Robert Oliphant wrote to Lord Bute on behalf of a 'Company of Gentlemen' who wanted 'to erect a large building for the spinning of Cotton in the same manner as is done at Matlock in Derbyshire'. It transpired later that James Kenyon was one of the gentlemen, and the Sederunt Book of the Commissioners of the Earl of Bute records among 'particulars respecting the Cotton Manufactory at Rothesay' an 'Agreement with Kenyon & Co dated 19th August 1778 for a lease of 99 years from Martinmas that year'.

It is later noted in this Sederunt Book that 'Yarn was spun on machinery erected in the old Lint Mill in 1779. The first yarn spun upon machinery in Scotland was in said mill. The Cotton mill at Pennycuick was built before the Mill of Rothesay, but yarn was first spun, as before mentioned, in the Old Lint Mill'.

Soon after the start of Rothesay's new enterprise Jas Stewart Mackenzie reported to Lord Bute:

> On the subject of the new Cotton Manufactory with a specimen of the Cotton thread made already at Bute, which in the opinion of the Glasgow people, is most excellent for various purposes of manufacture,

and it appeared that the island's claims were justified.

Effective may be the significant word in deciding priority, and certainly Rothesay's continued activity justified any pioneering claims as a forerunner of the tremendous expansion in the industry during the period from 1785 to 1795, with New Lanark's introduction to really large cotton-spinning operations in 1786 a highlight. Progress continued to be very rapid, with thirty-nine mills in 1796 and 120 in 1812.

Rothesay's cotton mill underwent several changes of management and direction. The mill was advertised for sale in 1785, six years after it was built, and it changed hands again in 1813, when it was bought by Kelly & Thom.

The period before the latter sale had been a difficult one, as

F   91 indicated in a letter of 4 November 1812 from Arch Moore, factor, to Lord Bute:

> I am sorry to acquaint your Lordship that the Cotton Mill Company have failed, and their affairs are in so bad a situation that the present prospect is nothing short of absolute bankcruptcy. Their failure will be attended with very serious consequences to the poor people in Rothesay in their employ. It has been a heavy business for the Company for many years past and the present situation of the Cotton Manufacturing trade has been the occasion of many failures.—The Cotton Mills I dare say will not sell for one third of what they cost, indeed I do not see how they can sell at all at present unless some favourable change takes place on the Continent.

In the event the prognosis appeared over-gloomy, but the change in ownership proved to be a notable step in the progress of Bute's cotton industry.

Robert Thom was a Greenock water engineer with enterprising ideas. He had been responsible for the remarkable planning and engineering of Greenock's water supply, and the reservoir on the hills above the town perpetuates his name as Loch Thom.

When Thom acquired the Rothesay mills, he was aware that they were totally dependent on a water supply that was inadequate for the expansion he had in mind. During the 1820s he constructed his famous series of water-cuts, nearly 7 miles of them, in an elaborate system designed to carry water from Birgidale and Mount Stuart on the east, and south-east, and Scalpsie and Quien on the west, to a dam at Loch Fad. Relics of these remarkable cuts, with their aqueducts and bridges, can still be seen at various parts of the island, including Ardscalpsie, Loch Fad, and Rothesay's Lade, Kirk Dam, and meadows, where the sluice which regulated the flow of water is prominent. These aqueducts, which were fully investigated in 1957, were similar to those in the hills above Greenock. John Ferrier made a full-scale study of Thom's water-cuts in Bute, and published his findings in the *Transactions of Glasgow Archaeological Society*. Many of the details of this excellent comprehensive report are fascinating, even on a non-specialist level.

Realising that an island with no mountains or rivers, and a rainfall that was significantly lower than the adjacent mainland, could not supply naturally the waterpower he needed for the expanding Rothesay cotton mills, Thom embarked on ambitious plans. Especially interested in hydraulics, he decided to rely completely on waterpower, advocating 'get water if you can, and be quit of these smoky and expensive engines'. His methods were based on the general principle of making the main storage dam as large as possible, diverting every available stream to the dam by a comprehensive series of aqueducts, allowing for auxiliary reservoirs to collect floodwater during spate as a reserve against drought, and providing sluices to control the water, thus avoiding waste and damage by flood.

Thom put forward sound practical ideas for converting natural streams to aqueducts, capturing the waters of other streams, following the contours of the ground, and narrowing the aqueduct, and steepening the gradient when rock outcrop was encountered.

His general plan was to increase the flow of water into Loch Fad (raising the level 15ft higher than at present), and water was brought from the east, south and west of the island into Loch Fad and so to the cotton mills. The storage capacity of the loch was more than doubled. A sketch plan dated 1827 gives some idea of the aqueduct system. The whole ingenious enterprise was an outstanding success, doubling the waterpower for the mills, and allowed a considerable expansion in output and numbers employed for many years. Possibly the biggest setback to his plans followed the diversion of the Scoulag Burn into the cut at White Lodge, which cut off the water supply to Mount Stuart and led to a prolonged legal battle with the Marquess of Bute.

Robert Thom's contribution to Rothesay's cotton industry

was outstanding, and something of his pioneering genius in surveying and carrying out work, without accurate maps and instruments, may be realised from the fact that the first Ordnance Survey of Bute is dated 1863, fifty years after the cuts were started. John Ferrier pays tribute to Robert Thom's 'concern with the social aspects of industry', and tells how he influenced Robert Owen's New Lanark experiments in labour relations. He also observes that 'nothing comparable to the cuts had been built since the Romans brought their aqueducts into Great Chester and Dorchester'. The final estimate is of 'a man of genius who over a century ago faced the present-day problems of urbanisation, rural depopulation, and atmospheric pollution'. Robert Thom died at Ascog in 1847, and his memorial stone can be seen in the High Kirkyard of Rothesay, where he is buried.

The cotton mills were of vital importance to Rothesay's economy during the major part of the nineteenth century. In 1801 there were 700 cotton workers and 200 weavers, and children worked in the mill from 6 am to 7 pm; and by the 1820s the cotton industry was employing well over 1,000 workers. By 1840 one mill alone employed over 350 people, and there were 23,440 spindles. It was recorded that 'workers in this mill are very healthy, work according to the regulations of the Factory Bill. About 150 of the youngest attend well-taught school in the evening, and their morals are not inferior to those of the rest of the population, a circumstance that is not a little owing to the excellent discipline kept by the manager'.

In this same year it was noted that a power-loom factory employed eighty-five hands. The boom continued well past the middle of the century, and although by 1860 the peak had been reached and the decline had set in, there was no sudden recession. As late as 1872 records show that over 200 people were employed in the weaving mill of A. & J. McKirdy, while the Broad Croft Spinning & Weaving Mills had over 400 employees, making a total of well over 600 still working in the industry.

Yet only ten years later the peak of five mills had been reduced to one, and it could be said that by 1882 the cotton industry in Bute was virtually extinguished. Various reasons contributed to the decline: perhaps the main reason was that the introduction of steam power necessitated the use of heavy machinery unsuitable for the Bute building, but geographical factors and changing patterns of transport and distribution were also contributory.

As the local cotton industry declined, there was a movement of workers away to other mills, mainly in Lanarkshire, a significant factor in the island's declining population. There are relics of the vanished industry in the remains of the old weavers' cottages, and the shell of the first 1779 cotton mill, which, after being long disused, was destroyed by fire in 1955.

OTHER INDUSTRIES

Some industries besides cotton are now only memories. *Fowler's Commercial Directory* of 1834 recorded that hundreds were employed in the cotton industry, shipbuilding, and the distillery. There were ropeworks in Rothesay, a tannery, small nail- and candle-making factories, and several cooperages employing thirty-four hands to make over 15,000 herring barrels a year. At one time a sawmill employed over forty men, while there were several market gardens and a meal mill.

There was a busy brick and tile works at Kingarth that lasted for over 60 years and at one time had great economic importance for the south end of the island. Founded in 1849 on the initiative of the Marquess of Bute, the works had varied success as fortunes rose and fell, but at the peak period of the second half of last century over twenty men were employed, and the annual output could exceed $1\frac{1}{4}$ million tiles and half a million bricks. Apart from regular local use, particularly on drainage schemes, thriving trade with the Highlands, Islands, and Northern Ireland was carried on. The final closure in 1915 was partly caused by lack of demand, and partly because of the exhaustion of suitable local clay seams.

The mainly unsuccessful experiments in mining coal, and the presence of a ruined salt kiln at Ascog, are reminders of an associated enterprise. The idea was to use local coal for boiling seawater for the manufacture of salt, but the scheme was soon abandoned because of various difficulties, including the poor supply of local coal.

FORESTRY

Although as an island Bute is reasonably well wooded, forestry is relatively unimportant compared with agriculture. Bute Estate is responsible for nearly all forestry on the island, and has its own sawmill at Piperhall. Apart from the extensive wooded area of Mount Stuart estate, there are over 800 acres of plantation in the south end of Bute. A heavy toll of wood-land was taken during the two wars, and, while there has been much replanting, a further reduction was caused by the havoc of the great gale of January 1968, which destroyed in one night nearly half the Bute Estate's coniferous timber, and over the island laid waste thousands of mature trees, necessitating a clearance operation that seems likely to continue at least until 1974.

It is difficult to estimate the present position exactly because of recent destruction and clearing, but previously it had been noted that Bute had 1,200 acres of conifers and 4,000 acres of broad-leaved trees, mainly birch, oak, beech and sycamore. At present approximately thirty men are employed in forestry on the island.

TOURISM

This is now the island's main source of income, and obviously its development must remain a high priority in any planning. On the evidence of occupation figures for 1970, 640 people, amounting to over 22 per cent of the working population, were employed in hotels and restaurants, while obviously a fair proportion of the 480 employed in shops, and others employed in transport, etc, are also dependent on the holiday trade. These figures do not include the additional employment of casual labour during the height of the holiday season.

Rothesay has been a holiday resort for over a century and a half, and the pattern has changed significantly over these years. Probably the peak period was reached between 1880 and 1910, when Glasgow's growing prosperity, and the fashion of residential family holidays, brought tourist booms to most Clyde Coast resorts, of which Rothesay was perhaps the most popular and prominent. By the time of World War I a different pattern and a different clientele—less wealthy, more working class—was noticeable. Between the wars there were alternating periods of prosperity and recession, and although Rothesay retained its popularity, there was a tendency towards shorter holidays, and, significantly, a growing popularity for weekend and day trips. After World War II Bute entered a difficult period of decline and adjustment, for which different reasons have been given, the most valid being the tremendous growth of foreign holidays and the restriction of the Clyde steamer sailings. At present much thought is being given to ways of promoting and reviving interest in the island as a holiday centre, and also as a conference centre, and, as will be seen, Bute is still exceptionally well equipped to develop a thriving tourist industry.

NEW INDUSTRIES

Apart from the various distributive and service trades, mainly centred in Rothesay, which have significance in the town's combined role of business and commercial centre, market town and holiday resort, several new industries have been introduced, and there are some signs of a limited but significant resurgence of industry in Bute. The present Marquess of Bute is strongly in favour of this development, and takes a prominent and active part in more than one of the new enterprises.

Bute Looms developed from the idea of a previous marquess, who started, in 1947, a handcraft home industry for ex-servicemen, specialising in handweaving and the making of deerhorn articles. The present marquess enlarged the enterprise into a commercial undertaking under the name of Bute Looms. Handweaving remained the speciality, but in a much more fashion-conscious way, and with a completely modern approach. In 1970 there was a general change to power looms, which proved much more versatile, but five handlooms were retained for the specialised trade. The company is now well known internationally, and has proved most enterprising and efficient. Specialising in the manufacture of cloth and fibre, with a sister company making garments from the cloth, Bute Looms have in their short history made a real impact on the fashion world, and despite the recent difficulties in this trade generally, the outlook is promising.

Two of the newer industries in Rothesay have a strong connection with the great fishing days of Bute. Ritchie Bros, the island's kipper and smoked salmon specialists, working from the famous Barr's kippering premises known to generations of prewar holidaymakers, have in fifteen years built up a business with a worldwide market that involves processing 100 stone of kippers a week in season, and smoking up to 100 salmon a night at peak periods.

AGRICULTURE, FISHING, AND INDUSTRY

Rothesay's newest industry is the development of the scallop market, mainly for export, by Rothesay Sea Foods Ltd, who employ as many as seventy and have seventeen fishing boats, five of them Rothesay-based, under contract.

A new clothing factory, Langan's, was opened in 1969, operating from a disused church in the High Street, and employing over thirty people. Cut cloth is made up into children's and other garments including duffel coats.

Bute Pottery, created by Mr Alexander Sharp, who trained in St Ives under Bernard Leach, the pioneer of modern studio pottery, started in 1960, using the old premises of Charles Sweet, a well known Rothesay photographer. The pottery is of high quality and is sent away to other shops, besides being available to the visitor to Bute.

In contrast to the newer industries, some of Bute's long-standing enterprises continue to prosper, having adapted themselves successfully to changing times. The two boatbuilding yards on the island, McIntyre's at Port Bannatyne and Bute Slipdock at Ardmaleish Point, provide excellent examples. The family business of McIntyre's, now under the control of Donald McIntyre, has been a prominent Port Bannatyne landmark for generations. In addition to building boats, especially the famous yachts, the firm is now concerned with diverse activities, including hiring, repairing, jetty construction, and Rothesay pierhead enterprises, and employs over forty men. One of the more exotic activities involves the conversion of the *Joven Teresa* to a yacht for a Scottish whisky magnate. The Ibiza ship, with its tall masts and striking figurehead, provides a colourful sight in the harbour.

Bute Slipdock still concentrates mainly on boatbuilding, and is internationally famous for its ocean-going yachts. A recently completed contract was for a Sudan hospital-boat with fibreglass hull. At present about twenty men are employed.

Lister's nurseries, established for over 100 years, have

EMPLOYMENT FIGURES FOR 1961

	Males employed	Males unemployed	Per cent unemployed
Island of Bute	2,000	230	10·3
Rothesay Burgh	1,590	190	10·7

	Females employed	Females unemployed	Per cent unemployed
Island of Bute	1,180	60	4·8
Rothesay Burgh	970	40	3·9

	Total employed	Total unemployed	Per cent unemployed
Island of Bute	3,180	290	8·4
Rothesay Burgh	2,560	230	8·3

OCCUPATIONS ON THE ISLAND OF BUTE 1970

	Number employed	Per cent
Agriculture	150	5·2
Forestry	30	1·0
Building Trades	300	10·3
Transport and Communications	240	8·4
Boatbuilding	60	2·1
Local Authorities	250	8·5
Professional, clerical, etc	250	8·5
Shops and Warehouses	480	16·6
Hotels and Restaurants	640	22·1
Fishing	40	1·4
Manufacturing	220	7·5
Unemployed	240	8·4
Total Active Population	2,900	100·00

specialised in the growing of dahlias, and their varieties are known throughout the gardening world.

The Scottish Milk Marketing Board's creamery was opened in 1954, receiving milk from over fifty Bute farms to an annual total of over over 1 million gallons, much of which is made into cheese for national distribution. About fifteen people are employed.

Of the remaining sources of local employment, the various aspects of the building trade account for close on 300 workers, a number that should be maintained during Rothesay redevelopment programme; while about 250 are directly employed by local authorities, and about the same number come under the heading of professional, technical, and clerical employment.

A 1972 estimate indicates that a total of slightly under 3,000 people are regularly employed on the island, and that there was a winter unemployment figure of over 250, approximately 8½ per cent. A significant improvement is noticeable during the summer season, but the male unemployment figure of over 10 per cent is exceptionally high, and as a sizeable number in this class are over the age of fifty, improvement is difficult to achieve. Another noteworthy feature is that over 10 per cent of the working population are employed outside the island, and without this factor the local unemployment figures would be even higher.

The problem of unemployment remains a serious one in Bute's development of a satisfying way of life.

6 TRANSPORT & COMMUNICATIONS

COMMUNICATIONS are an essential part of the life of any community, and with an island like Bute the development and maintenance of connections with the mainland are vital. Although the coming of air transport has revolutionised the communications of many Scottish islands, it has had no effect at all on Bute, and, perhaps surprisingly, there appears to be no immediate prospect of any air service.

Obviously the provision of a road bridge, advocated for several decades now by some enthusiasts but not yet a practical prospect in the near future, would dramatically alter the transport picture, but at present as in the past, sea transport is still the core of the island's system of communications.

SEA TRANSPORT

It has been pointed out that the first visitors to Bute were seafaring men who discovered the island as a separate entity, and not, as it has become to be thought of recently, as a part of the mainland that happens to be cut off by a narrow neck of water. But geographical considerations apart, Bute has always been closely concerned with sea transport, and even in local communication the island's sea transport has remained more important than any form of road transport. Only the emergence of the long-considered bridge over the Kyles would finally change this balance.

From early times Rothesay had a pier and harbour, while for centuries a number of smaller ports and harbours existed around the shores of the island. Port Bannatyne, Kerrycroy, Kilchattan, Straad, Kilmichael, and several other little ports and ferry points had their boats and harbour. Many different seagoing vessels have brought welcome and unwelcome visitors to the island. The boats that the first Neolithic men used to sail from the south to this new green isle can only be imagined, while even the coracles of the early Celtic missionaries are shadowy craft, although the Viking ships that followed are of a more definite pattern. The warships of the Scottish kings or English 'Protectors' have their place in the records, but it is only with the emergence of the first of the sailing ships, and then the steamers, that sea transport directly affected the communications of the majority of the inhabitants of Bute.

Kings and nobles had imported luxuries to the island, and there was some trade in certain commodities; the ferries from Kerrycroy to Largs, or Kilmichael to Argyll, transported animals and the occasional traveller, while there was considerable coming and going to the island at the time of the ancient fairs and markets. The old records show that almost every saint's name was celebrated by a fair day, and on those occasions the ferries were kept busy.

Before the building of the Rothesay pier the ferry between Kerrycroy and Largs was probably the most important link in communications with the mainland, but as the harbour was developed, the other ferry traffic declined. In 1755 the pier at Rothesay was extended, and in 1787 a new pier was built, and, after further extensions, the present pier was built in 1822, and the unique double harbour was preserved.

From the early years of the nineteenth century Bute's sea transport entered a period of great expansion. In 1804 it was on record that mainland communications were mainly dependent on a ferry service from Rothesay to Ardyne, and a packet service between Rothesay and Greenock. The story after that is one of ever-increasing traffic from Glasgow's Broomielaw to Rothesay; from the days of the *Comet* to late Victorian times those little steamers, at first privately owned and later company-managed, became an exciting and integral part of the everyday life of Bute and the places of the Clyde.

Some indication of the recognised importance of sea transport to the island is given in the old council records. As early as 30 June 1665 a burgh minute indicates that 'the whole inhabitants [were] obliged to contribute towards repairing the harbour'. In the *Glasgow Mercury* of 9 March 1786 the following advertisement was inserted:

> An undertaker wanted. The magistrates and council of Rothesay, in the island of Bute, intend to erect a new pier of about 200 yards long and 25 feet broad, for the further improvement of the harbour, persons willing to undertake the executing this work will please to give their proposals without delay, to the magistrates, who are ready to point out to them the situation in which the pier is to be carried, the method in which it is to be constructed, and to satisfy as to any other particulars necessary to be previously known before making out estimates. The undertaker will have the privilege of quarrying stones and taking other material from the town's grounds, where it is believed a good freestone quarry can be obtained.

In the following year, an extract of July 1787 records:

> Council petitions the Convention of Royal Burghs for assistance in rebuilding the quay, on the ground of poverty of the burgh.

The Convention granted £400 to the burgh in 1788.

A minute of 3 November 1791 indicates another problem involving sea transport:

> Memorial sent to the Postmaster-General anent the carriage of mails, narrating that the two men who had hitherto been paid £11–6s each for carrying mails in a boat from Greenock to Rothesay three times a week, had given up the employment, and suggested an advanced rate of payment.

An item of 8 February 1813 indicates a new development in sea transport with obvious relevance to Rothesay shipping and fishing:

Letter from General Campbell, M.P., relative to the completion of the Crinan Canal, and memorial by the Council thereanent, in which it is stated that there are 109 registered vessels belonging to the port of Rothesay, representing a tonnage of 5000, besides a number of craft under fifteen tons.

On 10 May 1816 the first mention of steamboats is made in the Council minutes:

> The magistrates and Council agree to accept of five guineas from each of the steamboats, *Rothesay Castle*, and *Dumbarton Castle*, as a composition for harbour dues, for twelve months, and authorise the magistrates to make as advantageous a bargain as they can with the master and owners of any other steamboats coming to the place.

The making of an 'advantageous bargain' caused some difficulty later. However, the Rothesay authorities were keenly aware of the importance of the harbour in the light of new shipping developments. On 20 November 1820 it was noted:

> Scheme laid before the Council by the Marquis of Bute, whereby he proposed to raise £5000 for the improvement of the harbour; £4000 to be borrowed from the Commissioners for the issue of Exchequer Bills, and £1000 to be advanced by the Marquis. £2000 having already been raised by subscription, it was proposed that those sums be placed in the Marquis' hands, he being security for the £4000. By means of this advance £5000 could be laid out on the harbour, at no other charge than the payment of interest for twenty years. The meeting approved.

The contract for the new works on the quay was given in 1822, and the work proceeded according to plan. By 1829 it was noted that 'the steamboats which leave Rothesay daily are stated to be the George Canning, Ewing, Locheck, Maid of Islay, Rothesay, Inverary, Toward, and Dunoon Castle—eight in all'. The trouble foreshadowed fourteen years earlier on the question of harbour charges came to a crisis in 1830, when a minute of 14 June stated:

A dispute having arisen as to the rates charged at the quay for the steamers Superb, Ewing, and Locheck, belonging to Mr. David Napier, he refused to pay anything, whereupon the harbour master warned away the boats; upon which Mr. Napier raised an action of suspension in the Court of Session to try the right of the magistrates to levy dues; and they having taken the opinion of Counsel on the subject, were advised that the rates could not properly be enforced; whereupon it was resolved to compromise with Mr. Napier, and apply to Parliament for an Act for the harbour.

A year later, in August 1831, it was intimated that the Harbour Bill had received royal assent and become law.

By 1837 seven steam vessels were plying regularly to and from Glasgow. Among other activities they transported 6,000 tons of coal to the island, and they were vitally important to the growing cotton industry. The pattern of sea transport between Bute and the mainland was now firmly established, and the way was clear for the spectacular increase in passenger and freight traffic during the remainder of the nineteenth century. Bute's connections with Glasgow, Greenock, the Ayrshire coast, Cowal, the Argyll peninsula, and the islands of Arran and Cumbrae were extensive, providing an excellent service, and a high standard of regular and frequent communication. Rothesay was the key point, but for many years the other island piers at Kilchattan Bay, Port Bannatyne, and Craigmore, had their own share of sea traffic. Improvement in the island's internal road transport was largely responsible for the closure of these subsidiary piers. Port Bannatyne and Craigmore were not used after the 1930s, but Kilchattan Bay survived on a reduced scale until 1955.

Although much of the Clyde Steamer saga belongs to a later chapter, it is essential to record as part of the sea transport outline the enormous surge of Glasgow holidaymakers and day trippers who have for a century and a half visited Bute by boat, exerting a vital impact on the economy of the island. During the peak years between 1890 and 1910 this represented a spec-

Page 107 (*top*) Rothesay pier: the presence of a steamer at Rothesay pier has been a familiar sight for a century and a half; (*centre*) a favourite Clyde steamer: The *Duchess of Hamilton* was one of the most popular cruising steamers until 1971; (*foot*) last of the line: The *Waverley* is the world's last sea-going paddle steamer, and great efforts are being made to keep her in service as long as possible

Page 108 (*above*) Modern boats: Rothesay's modern cruiser-stern boats, successors to the old herring fishing craft, concentrate mainly on white fish; (*below*) yachts in Port Banna-tyne Bay: although the days of the great regattas have passed, yachting remains part of the Firth of Clyde scene

tacular movement of people. On the Glasgow Fair Friday and Saturday of 1894 it was estimated that twenty-five steamers carried over 30,000 holidaymakers to Rothesay, while in 1906 the forty-two Clyde steamers with their daily passenger capacity of 60,000 passengers must have transported over half a million day, weekend, and longer holiday visitors to the isle of Bute.

Despite the spectacular peak figures, the large-scale sea transport between Glasgow and Bute was not limited to a brief heyday, but has been a longstanding enterprise. In the 1860s there were thirty all-the-way steamers from Broomielaw, and even in the 1880s, when railway enterprise had won a large share of the Glasgow traffic, sea transport was still vital for the last lap from Greenock, Gourock, Craigendoran, or Wemyss Bay to Rothesay.

The shortening of journey time by using rail as well as steamer, and the consequent increase in carrying capacity, had an enormous effect on numbers travelling, and provided a great impetus and incentive to day trippers. The Glasgow–Wemyss Bay–Rothesay trip in particular, with its much advertised 90min journey and half-crown fare, was an important element in the popularising of Bute. Although in postwar years it became fashionable to talk in terms of decline, a study of passenger figures to Rothesay by sea still makes remarkable reading: a steady traffic of over 300,000 July and August visitors, with a peak annual figure of over 700,000 in 1955.

PASSENGERS DISEMBARKING AT ROTHESAY PIER DURING JULY AND AUGUST

1950	340,000	1956	350,000
1951	320,000	1957	350,000
1952	330,000	1958	345,000
1953	310,000	1959	325,000
1954	335,000	1960	305,000
1955	395,000		

Figures are not available for the period since 1960, but it is estimated that the numbers have continued to decline, as they had done in the last five years covered by the table. In the peak year of 1955 the total number of passengers disembarking was 709,000. Thus 56 per cent of the traffic is concentrated on the two busiest summer months.

CARS LANDED AT ROTHESAY PIER DURING JULY AND AUGUST

1955	2,600	1958	4,000
1956	3,000	1959	8,000
1957	3,500	1960	9,000

Although figures are not available for recent years it has been confirmed by the Traffic Manager of the Caledonian Steam Packet Company that in 1972 approximately 40,000 cars were transported on the Wemyss Bay–Rothesay crossings, consisting of 30,000 in the summer months and 10,000 in the winter. These statistics indicate that the car traffic across the Firth continues to increase greatly.

Apart from the time-tabled steamer services, a large amount of cargo was carried to and from the island by the small puffers, which by their character, adaptability, and resilience have earned a share in the lore and saga of the Firth of Clyde. Bute's local ferry services were to a great extent superseded by the steamers, but one or two lingered for a time, notably the ferry from Kilmichael in north-west Bute to Tighnabruaich. The old ferry house at Kilmichael is a reminder that within living memory there was a regular service across the Kyles at this point. The one surviving ferry, now improved and modernised, is between Rhubodach and Colintraive, connecting Bute with Argyll at the shortest point between island and mainland. Colintraive is one of the few ferries in Britain that is not subsidised; with its new motor-carrying vessels it provides an alternative to the Rothesay–Wemyss Bay car service.

The island's most significant feature has been the declining general steamer service, and the advent of specialised car-carrying vessels, which now have a virtual monopoly of the Rothesay–Wemyss Bay connection. A new Pier Terminal with modern facilities for tourists, yachtsmen, and motorists, was built in 1968, while it is expected that the imminent introduction of a roll-on, roll-off car-ferry service will complete the immediate transformation of this means of communication. At the moment sea transport is as vital for Bute as it has ever been.

LAND TRANSPORT

To a small island surrounded by sheltered waters, land transport was until the last century little more than an incidental accessory to passage by water. The old moor-roads between farms, and the connecting rough roads to ports or ferries, were the only forms of orthodox land communication. There were occasional attempts to improve and regularise routes on the island, and in the town of Rothesay some consideration was given to the conditions of the streets. As early as 1665 a Town Council minute stipulated that 'all persons admitted burgesses to contribute a certain proportion towards paving the public streets'. Incidentally it was over a century before those streets were given identity. An extract of 30 August 1768 states: 'The streets of Rothesay having no names, the following are given: Castle Street, High Street, Watergate, Princes Street, Montague Street, Gallowgate, New Vennel, Ladeside, Store Lane, and Old Vennel'. Most of these streets are still in existence 200 years later, with the original names retained.

According to Blain's history there had not been any public high roads made nor any bridge built in Bute before 1764. In that year the work was begun and carried on by a statute labour committee, the more opulent parties not working paying 6d a day for exemption, and the poorer classes 4d. The roads in Kingarth were superintended by Lord Bute's factor; those in the district of the town of Rothesay, and thence to the ferries of Rue and Kilmichael, by Mr Blain; and the Cummernoch district, from Rothesay to St Ninian's Point, by Stewart of Stewarthall and Mr Campbell of Springfield. This arrangement seems to have been adequate for the very limited roads programme. Little reference is made to this subject in council proceedings, although a minute of 8 February 1813 records:

> Archibald Stewart of Ascog, having consented to bear a proportion of the expense of carrying a road from the burgh round by Laigh Bogany and the bay of Ascog till it join the high road at the shore of Kerrycroy, the Council consent to it being taken through the town lands, and agree to defray a proportion of the expense.

Until about 1880 Bute does not appear to have had any form of regular public transport service by road. The nearest were ancient horse-drawn cabs, which could be hired, and wagonettes that carried the first holidaymakers from Rothesay to Kilchattan Bay, and from Port Bannatyne to the sandy bay of Ettrick. Around this time these wagonettes first began to adopt a regular timetable, and travel by road became a more predictable business.

ROTHESAY TRAMWAYS

Bute's first significant public transport service came with the opening of the tramway system in 1882, after some initial difficulties had been overcome. The Rothesay Tramways Company, which played a key part in developing the island's communications, came into being in 1879, with the aim of establishing a horse-drawn tram service from Rothesay's Guildford Square to Port Bannatyne. Considerable delays were caused in overcoming some local objections and pursuing the inevitable legal formalities; but once these problems were solved, track-laying and the construction of small horse cars in local workshops were accomplished quickly, and the first tram was ready to run by the summer of 1882. The trial run and official opening aroused great local interest, and the first procession of the four open-roofed horse-drawn cars made a brave sight. There may have been no crowned heads to mark the occasion, but provost, magistrates, and town council proved acceptable substitutes.

Allan Leach, Bute's former County Librarian, has described some of the interesting and amusing episodes of the early days of Rothesay's tramway system in a fascinating study published in the 1969 volume of Buteshire Natural History Society's *Transactions*. Apparently the directors of the new company, excited by the success of the initial trials, immediately established a public service without official permission from the Board of Trade, whose representative demanded an immediate safety inspection, resulting in the discovery that the cars were 5in wider than allowed by the order. The Company's reaction was to saw 2½in off each side of the footboard, and then go ahead with the service.

During most of the day one car ran from each terminus at 15min intervals, the complete journey from Rothesay to Port Bannatyne being allotted half an hour, although there was scope for considerable reduction according to circumstance. As Mr Leach points out:

> Crews (and horses) ate while on duty, and were expected to take their tea between arriving at the terminus and leaving on the next journey. Obviously if time could be made up on the outward trip, then a longer break could be taken and the return journey still begin on time. Some horses knew this as well as their drivers, and one in particular had the reputation that when the other end of the journey represented time to enjoy a nosebag he would set off from Rothesay as though the furies were after him, and given the chance could reach Port Bannatyne in ten minutes.

An achievement of that first summer was the twelve cars' carrying in one day, the Glasgow holiday, no less than 5,200 passengers.

Among the problems of the company's early years were the competition of rival horse-brake organisations, the delays caused by the single-track system, and the deficiencies of the first open cars. The first threat of damaging competition had come from a Port Bannatyne man who operated a local service of horse-buses. After a preliminary offer of £300 by the tram-way company in exchange for a suspension of the horse-bus enterprise had been refused, an agreement was reached some months later for the withdrawal of the horse-buses, presumably after an increased offer. This arrangement did not deter a Rothesay man, John McMillan (a name that was to become well known in Bute transport enterprise), from introducing five horse-brakes on a service that was not only a direct chal-lenge to the tramway timetable, but forced them to take part in a fare-cutting war lasting over a year.

The single-track posed difficulties, as initially there were only four or five passing points over the whole route, including the termini at each end. The company, however, tackled this problem promptly, and within a year the *Rothesay Express* reported that a number of additional loop-lines had been constructed at strategic places, and that there was now prac-tically no delay at these passing points.

The first cars had not satisfied either passengers or company, and the addition of new strongly built cars, and the rebuilding of existing ones, helped to provide an all-year-round service, with open roofs for summer travel and closed roofs for local winter use. The company was thus ready to start its second summer service in 1883 with fourteen satisfactory cars (ten open and four closed), a team of thirty-eight horses, and a greatly improved loop system; and this was to be the pattern for the remaining 20 years of horse-drawn trams.

The timetable for the second season was an improvement, the normal standard being a 7min frequency during most of the day, with additional cars as required at rush periods, or on a steamer's arrival at the pier. At the height of the summer season there could be a peak service of cars every 2–3 min. In each of the first two summer seasons, comprising the months of June, July, and August, over 200,000 passengers were carried, the 1883 figures topping a quarter of a million for the three months, and the line was already a distinct success. By 1890 the total mileage reached was over 400,000; in 1895 over 600,000; and in 1901, the twilight year of the horse-drawn tram, the figure had risen to 700,000 miles. The 1890s, as in other Bute holiday enterprises, marked the peak of the success.

Electrification of the line had been mooted for a year or two before the enlarged company, no longer exclusively local, began to make concrete plans towards the changeover, but, before that, the single-track system was replaced by stretches of double-track working. Ideas were also mooted for extension of the line to Ettrick Bay, and for lines to Scalpsie and Kilchattan Bay. The latter proposals, which involved planning for a steam railway, lingered for some years before being finally abandoned, but the idea of an Ettrick Bay extension, after several setbacks, became a reality in 1905.

The electrification was accomplished in 1902, during a period of great activity, and some remarkable improvisation between the months of February and August. The first stage was the withdrawal of the horse-trams and the temporary substitution of a horse-bus service. When the new track was completed in May, the horse-cars returned, with wheels modified to suit the new gauge, and maintained the service until mid-August, when the electrified line was ready. The ten electric trams, which were subject to a speed limit of 10mph covered the Rothesay–Port Bannatyne journey in a quarter of an hour. In accordance with previous practice the summer cars were supplemented by five enclosed saloon cars for use in winter. With the full implementation of the electric system, the horse-trams were sold, and the end of a minor saga reached.

The first full season of electrification in 1903 had its ups and downs. Public objection to the excessive and dangerous speed of trams (15–20mph was alleged) was increased by several accidents, including a fatal one in August. It was pointed out, however, that even in the first month of the earlier horse-drawn service in 1882 there had been a fatal accident. The speed controversy lingered for some time, but this and other complaints were offset by the increased traffic and general popularity of the tram service. When the Ettrick Bay extension was opened in 1905, the company began a large-scale campaign to popularise the attractions of their new terminal point. Evening excursions, sports events, musical concerts, dances, and various competitions were organised.

For the rest of the tramways story the accent is on consolidation rather than development. The fleet of tramcars never exceeded twenty-two, but for years the trams had the virtual monopoly of the island's public transport, and maintained an impressive service. Perhaps the most interesting and most popular vehicles on the line were the three long 'toast-rack' trams, which were designed to carry eighty passengers, and on busy occasions were known to accept over 100. By the mid-1920s the opposition from privately owned motor-buses was serious enough to worry the company, who virtually admitted defeat by operating their own motor-buses, which eventually replaced trams on the winter services. From 1931 the tramway was only a summer service, and although greatly enjoyed by the holiday visitors, could not withstand for long the ever-growing opposition of the buses, and the final tram left Guildford Square on a last run on 30 September 1936. So ended an impressive record of 54 years, covering 20 years of horse-drawn trams, and a further 34 under electrification.

As an island enterprise Bute's tramway system had many unique features. Understandably it was the only one of its kind on a Scottish island, and perhaps the nearest parallel is the longer-lasting and better known Isle of Man service. Rothesay Tramway's main contribution to transport development was to span the half-century prior to the full expansion of the island's motor transport. But to many a native of Bute or West of Scotland holidaymaker the memory that remains is of that unique section of track between Port Bannatyne and Ettrick Bay, where the rails were not laid on a road but on a sleepered track across fields of flowers, in open country with magnificent views.

During the heyday of the horse-trams, places like Craigmore, Ascog, and Kerrycroy, the smaller resorts south of Rothesay, had two-horse brakes as their main form of transport, while Kilchattan, which despite all the plans never got its tramway extension, had the distinction of being served by coach-and-four. A. Cameron Somerville describes these vehicles as 'large, high and gaily painted affairs, which had names and on which passengers mounted to their seats by ladders. They were driven by coachmen as attractive as their coaches, for they wore yellow breeches, scarlet coats, top-boots and tile hats, and so certainly added colour and interest to the landscape'. Mr Somerville does not add that these coachmen were sometimes as lordly in manner as in appearance, and would think nothing of requiring their passengers to dismount and walk up the steeper hills to rest the horses!

Around the turn of the century the smaller horse-bus companies merged under the partnership of MacKirdy & MacMillan, well known names in the island's transport story, and continued to maintain for a number of years the timetables of the horse-drawn services, adding a variety of interesting summer excursions around and across the island. As everywhere else, the coming of the motor car changed transport radically, and although Bute was slower to respond than most places on the mainland, the revolution was merely delayed. The first privately owned motor car reached the island in 1905, and in 1909 the first motor-bus service ran from Rothesay to Kerrycroy. This was followed by a growing fleet of charabancs and buses, and although the coach-horse tours continued right on until the 1930s, the reason by then was holiday novelty rather than practical transport.

When the Rothesay Tramway Company was taken over by the Scottish Motor Transport Company Ltd in 1934, plans for a near-monopoly of public road transport on the island were under way. Before the abandonment of the tram service, the company bought out all but one of the private bus operators, and took control of all local services except Rothesay's Canada Hill service, which remained independent. This pattern has remained, with almost all the island bus traffic being handled by the Western SMT Company, which provides a fairly adequate local service, augmented in the summer season, and supplemented by tours and excursions around the island. Rothesay's taxi-cab service is well organised, and compares very favourably with those of most towns of its size.

Bute's roads are very good, and surface improvements have maintained a high standard, which has helped to cope with the increase in traffic resulting from the presence of more locally owned cars, and also the augmented car-ferry service to the island. Except for the July–August holiday period, and particularly in the narrow streets of central Rothesay, congestion has not so far become a major problem; and a modest but very attractive network of roads facilitates local communication, and allows visitors to see most of the attractive corners of the island.

The possible construction of a bridge joining Bute to the mainland at the Narrows near Colintraive would have considerable impact on island traffic. It is probable that despite the long distance from Glasgow to Colintraive by road, such a bridge would bring an invasion of day trippers who have previously been deterred by the inconvenience and high charges of ferries. It is possible that the existing island road system might be swamped, and indeed the whole character of Bute changed. As will be seen later, there are opposing views on the question of a bridge, but from the point of view of transport such an event would bring much more radical change than the present pattern of steadily increasing seasonal car-ferry traffic.

There is no airport on the island. At different times pleasure flights have been sponsored from Ettrick Bay, particularly during the period when this part of the island was being promoted as a developing holiday centre, but there has been no regular air communication. A Hovercraft service between Rothesay and Largs on the Ayrshire coast was in operation for several summers, the last being 1971, but there appeared to be insufficient demand, and a decision was taken not to resume the service in 1972. On announcing the Hovercraft's withdrawal the Caledonian Steam Packet Co stated that the craft was unsuitable for weather conditions prevailing on the Clyde; but it is also true to say that the service did not appeal as a means of passenger transport to Bute, and was used mainly as a novelty excursion vessel.

Bute was the setting for an early experiment in aviation. This was carried out by a blacksmith, A. B. Barr, who in September 1910 attempted to fly in a 29ft wingspan monoplane with a vertical air-cooled engine. Although the attempt was unsuccessful, and the plane was never airborne, its engine was stored for many years in Rothesay, and is now in Glasgow's Kelvingrove Museum.

NEWSPAPERS

Rothesay is one of only four island towns in Scotland where newspapers are published, the others being Stornoway in Lewis, Kirkwall in Orkney, and Lerwick in Shetland. Rothesay's *Buteman* has had a long and distinguished history, since its first issue of 13 December 1854, which is displayed in the Bute museum. Although it was not the first newspaper on the island, its predecessors were spasmodic and short-lived. The *Rothesay Advertiser* was founded in 1847 by the postmaster of Rothesay, Duncan McCorkindale, and survived for only four editions. Some years later in 1852 John Wilson, bookseller and compiler of *Wilson's Guide*, a commercial directory of the town, introduced the *Rothesay Journal*, which lasted for nineteen monthly issues.

The *Buteman*, destined to have a much longer existence,

appeared at fortnightly intervals in its very early stages in 1854, but after a few issues became a regular weekly newspaper, a pattern that has continued for well over a century. Nine years after the *Buteman's* appearance the first issue of the *Rothesay Chronicle* was published, and these two newspapers coexisted for over 50 years until their amalgamation in 1924 under the title of *The Buteman and West Coast Chronicle*. A third newspaper, the *Rothesay Express*, was founded in 1877, and it also had a long career extending into the 1950s before publication was suspended. For over 30 years, until the *Chronicle* went out of business just before World War I, Rothesay had three flourishing weekly newspapers.

Just before the advent of World War II in 1939 the *Buteman* and the *Rothesay Express* amalgamated under Bute Newspapers Ltd, with John Mackenzie as manager. The two newspapers continued to function as separate publications, one at the weekend and the other in mid-week, until 1953, when the last issue of the *Express* was printed. Since that time the *Buteman* has been the sole newspaper, and caters not only for Rothesay and the island of Bute but the other islands in the county and an extensive area of the mainland, including the Kyles of Bute and Loch Fyne. The present sales of the *Buteman* average 5,500 weekly, quite a remarkable figure in relation to the island's 1971 population of less than 8,000, but an impressive subscription list extending far beyond the island and overseas must be taken into account.

The continuing publication of the *Buteman and Rothesay Express*, and the Mackenzie family's development of this newspaper business, is an impressive example of local enterprise. John Mackenzie, the veteran proprietor, who was born in 1887 and has had an active career of newspaper life spanning over 70 years, has described the origins of the family's long publishing record in *Country Editor*:

Father had come from his native Plockton, Ross-shire, with his widowed mother at the age of twelve, and after leaving school, was employed for some time as a grocer's boy. However he was ambitious, studied shorthand, became a member of the literary society, with its lectures and debates, and took a keen interest in the town's affairs.

In 1877 Mr. Blair of Greenock thought Rothesay required a mid-weekly newspaper in addition to the two published on Saturdays, and so the *Rothesay Express* came into being with Murdoch Mackenzie as editor. It flourished, and ten years later he became the owner, and established his own printing plant in Rothesay. His must have been a busy life, for besides editing the newspaper, and being correspondent for the *Glasgow Herald*, he owned a newsagent's and stationery business in Guildford Square, and was appointed writer to the Sheriff Court.

Murdoch Mackenzie and his son John shared between them over 70 years of service as the *Glasgow Herald*'s Rothesay correspondent, and the family's association with Rothesay newspapers has been even longer. Now in his eighties, John Mackenzie is still actively involved with the *Buteman*.

As a postscript to the newspaper record, perhaps mention should be made of a publication that appeared in the summers of 1896 and 1897 entitled *Clyde Programme* and claiming to be a 'Summer Paper for the West Coast'. Although it carried several news items and features, *Clyde Programme* was mainly concerned with advertising the various concerts, entertainments, and steamer excursions of those years when Rothesay's tourist boom was at its height.

POSTAL SERVICES

Rothesay provides the main post office and centre for the postal services of Bute, and until very recently the Kyles of Bute area of Argyll. Incoming mail used to be a shared enterprise between British Rail and MacBrayne's steamers, but withdrawal of the MacBrayne Kyles of Bute, Tarbert and Ardrishaig service in 1970 severed a long Royal Mail connection. Apart from the head office, Rothesay has three sub-offices, and there are six at other parts of the island, making a total of ten in all. The present practice is for two deliveries a day in town, and one in country areas. Motor vehicles are now used generally, except for town-centre delivery. The mail handled has varied very little according to the statistics covering the years between 1910 and 1955. There is, however, a substantial difference in the figures between summer season and off-season. In 1955 over 50,000 letters were posted during the latter, and nearly 90,000 during the season, and, remarkably, the figures for 1910 were substantially the same. Except for the peak holiday seasons of 1913 and 1920, when over 100,000 letters were posted, the pattern for the intervening years is fairly constant. Understandably in a holiday resort, deliveries during the season were at a lower level than postings, and off-season variations were less pronounced. A fairly sizeable increase in parcel deliveries has taken place—from approximately 1,200 to over 2,100, possibly due to an increase in mail-order business.

ROTHESAY POSTAL TRAFFIC 1910–55

	LETTERS POSTED		DELIVERIES	
	Non-season	*Season*	*Non-season*	*Season*
1910	52,147	94,838	43,419	62,220
1913	66,912	129,818	46,430	65,481
1919	43,951	76,538	37,983	52,482
1920	47,839	101,592	35,051	55,992
1925	42,018	75,543	38,433	53,245
1930	43,810	74,990	41,203	54,830
1940	44,800	75,600	49,870	65,600
1950	50,720	87,320	53,840	68,920
1955	51,413	88,510	55,655	59,184
		Parcels		
1910	926	1,083	1,197	1,623
1913	898	1,271	1,347	2,031
1919	776	942	1,309	1,806
1920	660	971	1,334	1,774
1925	769	934	1,165	1,820

	PARCELS POSTED		DELIVERIES	
	Non-season	*Season*	*Non-season*	*Season*
1930	841	1,089	1,258	1,364
1940	976	1,121	1,362	1,476
1950	925	1,210	1,980	2,090
1955	1,148	1,204	2,118	2,252

TELEPHONE AND TELEGRAPH

In common with other areas, use of the telegraph service has declined as the telephone service has been extended, although since 1956 Rothesay has been responsible also for the telegraphic traffic to and from the Dunoon area. The number of telephone subscribers has steadily increased to over 1,100, quite a high proportion in relation to population. Since the late 1950s a radio station built on the Bute moors has played an important part in providing additional ship-to-shore communication.

7 THE ISLANDER'S BUTE

THE history of any community provides its quota of paradoxes and apparent contradictions, but when an island with a long and distinguished history dating from ancient times, supplemented by a distinct share of medieval prominence, emerges after a brief spell of industrial activity as the centre of a spectacular wave of holiday tourism, it becomes difficult to define its true character. This dualism was noted as early as 1840, when a local minister described the town as one engaged in cotton-milling, herring-fishing, and agriculture, but since the introduction of steam navigation, fast becoming a 'fashionable watering-place'. With the passing of the cotton mills and the decline of the herring industry, the pattern changed, but something of the dualism remains, for although to many mainland folk Bute is thought of solely as a holiday isle, the residents have an active and varied life that has little to do with tourism, and might come as a surprise to those who see Rothesay only during those crowded midsummer months.

It may be unwise to attempt to describe or analyse the characteristics and traditions of a population that has changed even more drastically than most places in modern times. Of the present population less than 50 per cent were born on the island, and there are more incomers than natives among Rothesay's residents. Nevertheless there is a strong nucleus of Brandanes who remain deeply conscious of the island's heritage and culture, without in any sense living in the past; and the descendants of those who knew their dependence on the land

124

Page 125 (*above*) Old type Clyde Puffer: puffers of the type immortalised in Neil Munro's 'Para Handy' stories were regular callers with varied cargo at the piers of Bute; (*below*) *Glenfyne*—modern successor to the *Vital Spark*: coasters of this new type still unload cargoes at Rothesay and the other remaining Clyde piers

Page 126 (above) Rothesay: promenade and bandstand summer scene at the height of Rothesay's prominence as a holiday resort; (below) pier from Chapelhill: steamers at the pier still form a focal point for any view of Rothesay

and sea for their livelihood remain, in their modern fashion, farmers and fishermen of Bute.

POPULATION

Population figures for Bute reflect some of the striking changes in the way of life of the islanders over the past two centuries. Bute escaped the evictions and clearances experienced by the more northerly Highland and Island communities, but did not escape depopulation through lack of suitable occupations, nor the resultant emigration to the mainland and abroad. This factor has continued, occasionally featuring an increased exodus during periods of depression or unemployment, but until the last two decades keeping a fairly steady level, which has to some extent been countered by a corresponding influx of those people from the mainland who have decided to come to live on an island that attracts them. This might in some ways have appeared to be a happy solution, except for the fact that the incomers include a very large proportion of retired people, resulting inevitably in an ageing population trend with all its implications. (Bute has a larger percentage of old people than any other Scottish county, and the average age, which has been increasing steadily over the past thirty years, is now more than thirty-eight.)

When the exclusive pattern of agriculture and fishing was changed in the second half of the eighteenth century, the population of the parish of Rothesay increased from 2,658 in 1766 to 4,032 in 1790. By 1801 there were 3,760 people in the town of Rothesay, and a total of 6,106 on the island. In 1837 these numbers had further increased to 4,924 in Rothesay, and there were over 7,000 inhabitants of Bute.

Trade decline in the second half of the century was more than offset by the emergence of tourism, and Bute's continued expansion was reflected in population totals of over 8,000 in 1841, over 9,000 in 1851, over 10,000 in 1871, over 11,000 in

H

1881, and over 12,000 in 1901. The 1921 figure of 19,465 must be partially discounted, as the census was taken in June when the holiday influx had started. The true peak was probably represented by the 12,126 of 1931 and the 12,547 of 1951. Since the latter date decline has been denoted in decreases to under 10,000 in 1961, under 9,000 in 1966, and just over 8,000 in 1971.

The population, which had doubled between 1801 and 1951, has fallen in the ensuing twenty years from 12,547 to 8,141, a decrease of 35 per cent, and there are now less people on Bute than at any time since 1841. This rather sudden and dramatic decline, coupled with the additional factors of ageing population and above average unemployment rate, must give concern. Immediate causes of the depopulation trend were the sudden departure of the submarine squadron from the base in Rothesay Bay, and the increase in foreign holidays. Possibly Bute had depended overmuch on the presence of a naval establishment during the war and postwar years, but the ensuing loss of population and trade came as something of a shock. The change in the holiday pattern may prove to be a temporary feature, or it may be offset by increased leisure and holidays generally, but it will require action to redress the balance of population, which has led to the loss of over 4,000 inhabitants out of a total of 12,500 in 20 years.

The birthrate has fallen from 25 per 1,000 in the 1860s to less than half that number a century later, while the corresponding deathrate has fallen from 22 per 1,000 to approximately 14. Although these figures are fairly typical of the country as a whole, some of Bute's population statistics present a slightly unusual pattern. In the period from 1860 to 1910 the decline in deathrate compensated for the decrease in the number of births, allowing a small natural increase in population. From 1910 to 1950, however, the deathrate has exceeded the birthrate by an average of approximately 1·5 per 1,000, and during the years from 1930 to 1950 there was a natural loss of about 550,

THE ISLANDER'S BUTE

which was more than reversed by an increase in migration of over 2,000.

In 1951 an analysis by birthplace of the population revealed that only 38·6 per cent of the inhabitants had been born on the island, a steady decline from 1931 and earlier years. Now more than three out of every five are incomers, and among those who come to Bute from other parts of Scotland 20 per cent, nearly 4,000, predictably are from Glasgow; but a sizeable number, 1,375, or 7·1 per cent in 1931, and over double that number, 2,756, or 14·3 per cent in 1951, came from outside Scotland.

Within the island itself there has been no significant drift between town and country, and the only other notable feature is that the decline in Gaelic-speaking, a longstanding one for this island, has continued, and in 1951 only about 400 could speak the language, a number that has diminished even further in the following two decades.

POPULATION ON THE ISLAND OF BUTE SINCE 1801

	Island of Bute	Rothesay Burgh		Island of Bute	Rothesay Burgh
1801	6,106		1881	11,016	8,329
1811	5,824		1891	11,753	9,108
1821	6,599		1901	12,181	9,378
1831	6,830		1911	11,841	9,299
1841	8,078	5,789	1931	12,126	9,347
1851	9,386	7,104	1951	12,547	10,141
1861	9,483	7,227	1961	9,799	7,675
1871	10,094	7,800	1971	8,141	6,456

The 1921 census was taken during the holiday month of June, resulting in distorted figures that included several thousand visitors. No census was taken in 1941 because of World War II.

PERCENTAGE OF POPULATION OVER 65 YEARS OF AGE IN 1966

	Male	Female
Island of Bute	7·5	15·5
Rothesay Burgh	6·9	16·1
Scotland	4·4	7·0

129

THE ISLAND OF BUTE

MOVEMENT OF POPULATION TO AND FROM ROTHESAY IN PERIOD
1961–6

	Immigrants from	Emigrants to
Glasgow	300	130
Rest of Scotland	480	480
England and Wales	130	320
Overseas	110	—
Total	1,020	930

EDUCATION

The records of early education on the island of Bute are meagre and fragmentary, but extracts from general documents provide occasional reference to educational provisions, and a rough idea of the general development may be suggested. There was a school at Rothesay between 1557 and 1634, and mention is made in Grant's *History of Burgh Schools in Scotland* that:

> The council of Rothesay appear to have managed for a long time the Grammar School in the town but the presenting, placing, and giving commission to the schoolmaster belonged to Sir James Stewart of Bute and his predecessors.

Evidence suggests that this school in Rothesay had been in existence during the late sixteenth and early seventeenth centuries, and a minute from Kingarth Kirk Session Records of 1649 indicates that it was the only one in Bute, catering for the whole island. This Rothesay school was a public school as well as a grammar school, and although the founding date is unknown, the records of Rothesay Public School are continuously documented from 1655 onwards, one of the first entries on 15 May of that year being the appointment of the Town Clerk of Rothesay, Donald MacGilchrist, as schoolmaster.

During the seventeenth and eighteenth centuries there was a close association between church and school, and the church session had a strong control over local education. The original

130

Rothesay parish school had been a room in the bishop's palace, but there were accommodation problems, and 'In regarde that the Towne is desolate of one schoolhouse for the training and education of children', it was decided to build a new school on the south side of Castle Street in 1680, the dimensions being 20ft by 17ft, with thatched roof and earthen floor. The schoolmaster was Patrick Stewart, and it is noted that no house was provided for him when the school was built. Education was kept severely in its place, for at a time when the Tolbooth was roofed with slates from Kames, thatch was considered sufficient covering for the school. It was over 100 years, in 1798, before another school was to be built in Rothesay.

Kingarth parish's educational history is also a long one, and after that Kirk Session ordinance of 1649 a levy was made on landowners and cotters to pay a master for the school, which was opened in 1654. In 1677, after the nave of St Blane's church had fallen into ruin, the Session decided to build a new kirk, and establish a school within the kirk. As elsewhere, the Church Session was in control of school and schoolmaster until the 1872 Education Act. The provisions of earlier Education Acts were often unheeded in practice, with the payment of fees continuing to follow the previous 'use and wont' pattern.

During the eighteenth century there appeared to be some revival of interest in education; John, the third Earl of Bute, became tutor to George III, and although he later concentrated on politics, agriculture, and botany, he had at least a sympathetic approach to education, which was continued by his successors. It is on record in 1798 that a new school was to be built in Rothesay, at a total cost of £346 10s on a site provided free of charge by the Marquess of Bute, who also made a donation of £50.

In 1808 some attempt was made to establish a girls' school in the town, but again information is lacking. It is known, however, that around the years 1835–40 the island had fifteen schools of varying sizes and importance, and it was claimed that, with a total roll of over 900 pupils, there was 'scarcely a native youth who could not read or write'. Despite this claim it was not until the second half of the century that a real advance in Bute's education began. In 1861 there were definite moves to found an academy in Rothesay, and after a great deal of preliminary activity the idea was finally developed in 1867 when the trustees of Duncan Thomson, a native of the town, used his bequest of £6,500 to endow a first-class school in Rothesay, with the co-operation of, and in close association with, the East and West Free Churches. A year later the town council added £360, and six pupils were to be given free places in the school. Rothesay Academy was officially opened in 1870, and in 1874 its management was transferred to the new School Board. Another consequence of the important Education Act of 1872 was the building of a new public school in the town.

Rothesay's Academy played an important and impressive part in the island's educational development. During the original school's 84 years of existence it was considerably altered and extended at various stages, until it was destroyed by fire in a spectacular blaze in 1954. After an intermediary period of 4 years of improvisation, when alternative accommodation in church halls and other buildings had to be arranged, a modern four-storey school was erected on the site. The new building was ready by the end of 1958, and was officially opened in May 1959. As the only six-year secondary school in the county, Rothesay Academy has on its roll pupils from the islands of Arran and Cumbrae as well as Bute.

EDUCATION FIGURES FOR 1970

	Pupils	*Teachers*
Rothesay Academy	535	37
Rothesay Primary	549	16
Rothesay St Andrews	167	6
North Bute	69	3
Kingarth	26	1
Total	1,346	63

In addition to the Academy, which in 1970 had 535 secondary pupils, the Rothesay Primary School had 549 pupils, Rothesay St Andrews 167, North Bute 69, and Kingarth 26. With the closing of the rural schools at Kerrycroy and Ballianlay, Kingarth remains the only single-teacher school on the island, while the other four schools on Bute have a total staff of just over sixty teachers. The total number of pupils, 1,346, represents a decrease of approximately 200 in 15 years, but, in contrast to the general population estimate, the decline appears to have been arrested, and the immediate prospect is for a slight increase in the total roll. Of the secondary pupils around forty come from Arran and Cumbrae, lodging in Rothesay during term time. A number of parents in Arran have felt aggrieved about this aspect of their island's educational facilities, and over the years have pointed out that this attachment to Bute is an anachronism.

COUNTY LIBRARY SERVICE

Bute's library record is not undistinguished. As early as 1792 Rothesay Library had over 1,400 volumes, and there were several smaller libraries on the island. For many years the Norman Stewart Institute Library served local readers, until, in 1951, Bute Education Committee took over administration of the county library service, using the existing premises as a central library. A new library and headquarters is under construction in Rothesay, and branch library facilities are available outside the town.

RELIGION

The Benedictine monastery erected in Iona by the Abbot of Saint Columba took place in the same year as the disponing of St Blane's Church to Paisley. The Iona church was built for Reginald, Lord of the Isles, who, at that time, was Superior of

Bute. He also erected the monastery of Saddell for the Cistercian Order.

The Bishops of Sodor start in 1388 with John III and end in 1566 with John Carswell, Vicar of Kingarth and Kilmartin, and latterly Bishop of the Isles. 'Without doubt Bishops Allan and Gilbert (1283–1388) performed their priestly and episcopal offices in the Church of the Blessed Mary in Rothesay where their bones repose.'

John Muir in *The Church Architecture of Scotland* tells us that 'Lady Kirk, close upon the town of Rothesay, is also an interesting fragment of what seems to have been originally a structure of Norman date'. It was probably built around 1300 and converted into the mortuary chapel of the Stewards of Scotland about 1315. The site could have been that of an earlier Celtic church. On the floor among the grave slabs there is an effigy of a Norman warrior. There are two altar-tombs in the side walls, one with an effigy of a knight in armour, and one with a lady holding a child. The lady effigy seems to have been constructed with the wall, but in the other the effigy might have been let into the wall. The stone of the lady effigy is from the same quarry as that of the rybats and jambs of the building—the white sandstone of Bute. Hewison writes:

> The female figure is chastely executed in low relief in the same white stone. A gown and kirtle, with sleeves tightly circling the wrist, flows down with simple folds. The mantle, fastened upon the breast, sweeps down and appears with a running pattern of ivy upon it. Beyond her left arm reclines a babe, clothed in long robes. The hands, with fingers touching each other, lie upon her breast. The feet lie upon a rest, in shape not unlike an animal. The head reposes upon a pillow. The head is covered with a high cap or chaplet, from which a head-dress droops down over both ears to the shoulders.

The head-dress is in the fashion c 1270–1330. The base of the monument is divided into eight panels, within which is carved a female figure engaged on some office. Two of the figures display Celtic brooches.

The effigy is probably that of Alice, daughter of Sir John Erskine, first wife of Walter the Steward, for whom the mortuary was raised and the effigy placed in it by her husband, and the effigy of the knight might be that of Walter the Steward, erected about 1380 by Robert II his son. (Robert II was fond of tomb-making, and had his own made out of stone from England lying ready in St John's Church, Perth. There is an entry in his accounts for 1379 for a tomb for the 'father and mother of the king'.)

The present ruined Chapel of St Mary's is under the care of the Scottish Secretary, and the effigies can be seen with the picturesque detail that Hewison describes. The chapel belonged to the Cathedral of Sodor, the nave of which was removed in 1692 to make way for the parish church, which was also removed in 1795 to allow the present church to be built.

The manse was at Townhead or Kirktoun. In 1596 the manse is described as 'having the common gate of the church on the east side, the kirkyard on the south, the lands of Creagans pertaining to Donald Ballentyne on the west, and James Campbell land on the north parts'. In 1660 the manse was erected in the High Street. The Bishop's House was removed in 1785, when Bishop Street was made. It was the private residence of Patrick Stewart of Rosland, minister of Rothesay. Over the outer gateway were two stones, one of which bore the inscription 'Pax intrantibus, Salus exeuntibus' and the stone can still be seen at the foot of Bishop Street in the wall opposite the General Post Office.

The Cathedral Church was not the only place of worship in the parish, there being St Bride's on St Bride's Hill, now Chapelhill; St Columba's, probably on Columshill; St Michael's Chapel in the Palace; St Mary's near Kames; Kilmachalmaig; and probably Kilmichael in North Bute. In the mid-fifteenth century the vicar of Bute, Lord Nigel, was paid for conducting worship in St Bride's, and payment was made to another chaplain celebrating in the Castle of Bute.

During the sixteenth and seventeenth centuries the Kirk Session became all-powerful in supervising the life and morals of the parish. Charges covered a wide range of human behaviour, from being 'over-hilarious at a bridal ceremony' to the capital offence of witchcraft. Places in Bute associated with the latter crime include the Witches' Knowe near St Blane's, the witch's Craig in Glenvoidean, and the Fairies' Grotto at Ambrisbeg. Accusations of 'gangin' with the faryes' were frequently dealt with seriously by the Session, and the phrase 'away with the fairies' has survived in a lighthearted way.

In the late seventeenth and eighteenth centuries, witchcraft gave way to laxity in Sunday observance as a favourite misdemeanour. A proclamation of 27 June 1692 stated that 'It is enacted and ordained that no hostler or innkeeper shall sell any drink in tyme of sermon except to kirk persons', while the use of ferries on Sundays was prohibited except in emergency.

A different form of Sabbath-breaking—on a higher social level—is revealed in an early eighteenth-century record:

> Likeways Elizabeth Robisone, Lady Ascog, was delated for Sabbath-breaking and particularlie that upon the foresaid 27th of April last (1707) she did not onlie contribute to begin the foresaid Scandalous and Impious tumult in the Churchyard, but after it was thought to be over, did more than once with a loud voice Incite the said James Allan to challenge James Stewart and David Glasse to come up the brae to fight; and that when the Countess of Bute was passing by her at a distance, and in her chair, she—viz, the Lady Ascog—gave the saide Countesse sundrie very opprobious names, and that she was heard horridlie Imprecate the Earl of Bute, and his Familie, and saying that she hoped ere long to see the Earl of Bute's heart-blood.

The Session did not succeed in disciplining the bold Lady Elizabeth, however, even with the help of the Presbytery!

The session meetings nevertheless were of great importance. In the late 1600s the meetings were held at the kirks of Kingarth, Langalchorad, Kilchattan Mill, Clachanuisk, and other places. In December 1675 the nave of St Blane's Church fell into ruin, and a new kirk was completed in 1680. This Church, from the middle of last century, was called Mid Kirk, to distinguish it from St Blane's and Mount Stuart churches. The modern parish church, built in 1826, stood on the site of the Mid Kirk, but had to be pulled down after extensive damage during the storms of 1968.

In 1740 James Stewart, son of James of Kilwhinleck, was appointed minister of Kingarth. 'He was an eccentric and extravagant man with so pronounced a leaning to the exiled Stewart family that he preferred to pray for them instead of the king.' He was practically forced to resign in 1754, and six years later built the well known Stewarthall.

In Rothesay the pre-Reformation church was removed and the present structure erected in 1790 during the ministry of Dr MacLea, who, in direct contrast to Kingarth's eccentric, was an 'exceedingly able and successful parish minister'. He was appointed in 1765 and died in 1824, his monument lying behind the parish church. The tombstone of his predecessor, Hugh Campbell, is also in the churchyard.

The shadow of the Disruption hung over the nineteenth century, but in the long run unions of congregations more than compensated for new establishments. Successive unions of 1847, 1900, and 1929 led to the present Church of Scotland, which is now represented by the old parish church, The High Kirk of Rothesay, and eight other churches.

St Andrew's Roman Catholic Church serves more than one-tenth of the population, while the Episcopal, Baptist, Free Church, Salvation Army, and smaller sects are also represented.

HOUSING

Housing development in Bute has in recent years centred mainly on Rothesay, and very few houses have been built in rural areas of the island. During the nineteenth century there were some interesting enterprises outside Rothesay, perhaps the most notable being at Kerrycroy, a good example of the planned village of the time. In 1803 the Marquess had built new cottages and an inn on this part of his estate, but later the inn was converted to a school. The larger half-timbered houses were built in the 1890s. In more recent times a few new houses for agricultural workers were built at Kingarth, Croch-an-raer, etc, and there has been some modernisation of existing houses.

Private building also has been restricted, although a new enterprise in providing houses for private sale is under way at Ardencraig near Craigmore, and it is hoped that over a period of 5 years a total of eighty houses will be built.

There has been more need and demand for rehousing in the town of Rothesay, but expansion has been restricted to some extent by geographical considerations, particularly the steep ground on either side of Rothesay's narrow valley. The 1958 Development Plan for Bute estimated that 400 houses would need to be built in Rothesay, mainly to replace derelict or substandard buildings. By the time of the 1961 census seventy-five new houses had been completed at Minister's Brae, and in the following 10 years another ninety were built.

A new housing development, consisting of 140 houses, is under way in the Barone Road area, and there is a provisional plan for a further twenty-eight at Glebelands. The completion of this scheme should answer the problem of Rothesay's substandard houses.

About one-fifth of Rothesay's houses are provided by the local authority, and these are occupied by nearly one-third of the town's population. A sizeable proportion of private houses are still owned by absentees, census figures indicating a possible figure of 20 per cent.

LOCAL GOVERNMENT AND ADMINISTRATION

Bute is divided into three administrative units—the parishes of North Bute, the Parish of Kingarth, and the Burgh and Parish of Rothesay. The major town provides the county administrative centres, although in addition to a shared parliamentary representation Bute is linked to Renfrewshire for police and public health services, and to Argyll for national health services.

The sheriff court sits at Rothesay, having previously been part of the sheriffdom of Renfrew and Bute, but since 1946 part of the sheriffdom of Ayr and Bute.

The local authority in Rothesay is the town council, which comprises three representatives from each of the six wards to make a total of eighteen councillors, including a provost and three baillies who act as magistrates in the burgh courts. As in most Scottish towns there is a considerable general interest in council deliberations, and Rothesay has had its full share of excitement, argument, and feud, between opposing members on matters of strong local interest or personal opinion. The continuing source of interest in the town council proceedings is reflected in the local newspaper reports, which give close attention and full coverage to the more controversial proposals, points of order, and decisions.

PARLIAMENTARY REPRESENTATION

The history of Bute's parliamentary representation and political devolution has been a complicated one. After the Union of the Parliaments, arrangements relating to the governing of Scotland presented some complex features, with the general aim of effecting a reasonable compromise.

From 1707 until 1832 Bute and Caithness shared a member, each county having representation in alternate parliaments. The five Reform Acts of the nineteenth and twentieth centuries provided some major alterations to the immediate post-union arrangements. In 1832 Scotland's forty-five representatives were increased to fifty-three, alternate representation was ended, and Bute enjoyed the privilege of being a single constituency with its own member from 1832 until 1918.

In 1918 a redistribution of seats led to the amalgamation of Bute and North Ayrshire for the purpose of electing one member. The present representative at Westminster is Sir Fitzroy MacLean.

HOSPITALS AND MEDICAL SERVICE

Rothesay's Victoria Hospital, which was opened in 1897 and subsequently extended by the provision of a new wing in 1927 and a modern maternity unit in 1938, is an adequate and efficient centre for the routine needs of the island community. There are about twenty beds, an up-to-date X-ray department, and a small operating theatre. The recent pattern has been to arrange for mainland surgical treatment when possible, but the local hospital remains a vital part of Bute's health service. The nearby building, known as the Thomson Home, originally served as an institution for helping the poor of the parish, financed by Rothesay Academy's original benefactor, Duncan Thomson. Its present role is to provide a combined home and hospital for elderly residents. The Robertson-Stewart Hospital, planned to take cases of infectious diseases, now uses the majority of its beds for the chronic sick.

There are seven doctors on the island, all residing in Rothesay, four dentists, and two district nurses employed by the county council. A growing problem is the nursing care and service required by the large number of older residents.

WATER

Rothesay has two main water sources—Loch Ascog, which dates back to 1856 and was improved in 1939, and Dhu Loch, which has had several extensions since its first use in 1880. Loch Ascog supplies the lower and greater part of the town, and all the shore area from Ascog to Port Bannatyne, while Dhu Loch supplies the higher parts of Rothesay, and the Ballianlay and Straad communities on the west. Two small hill reservoirs supply Kilchattan and Kingarth.

Bute's water capacity exceeds 250 million gallons, adequate for present winter and summer needs.

ELECTRICITY AND GAS

Bute's electricity is supplied by the North of Scotland Hydro-Electric Board, by way of the Loch Striven power scheme. The use of electricity has continued to increase in recent years, and additional supplies are expected within the next decade.

The Rothesay Gasworks has a long history. In 1840 a company was formed to make and supply gas, and it was taken over in 1843 by the council, which continued as owner until nationalisation in 1949. The Scottish Gas Board now supplies over 2,500 customers in Rothesay from the local coal-fired gasworks, which is expected to be replaced eventually by a natural gas installation. General administration is organised from the Gas Board's western region headquarters at Paisley.

POLICE AND FIRE SERVICES

Since 1923 police services have been merged with those of Renfrewshire, and in 1949 full amalgamation made Bute a subdivision of the combined Renfrew and Bute Police Force.

Fire-fighting services are organised within the Western Area Fire Brigade, with headquarters at Paisley. Rothesay has a modern fire station.

SOCIETIES

Bute is exceptionally rich in thriving local societies, which play an important part in the life of the community. Pride of place must go to one of the oldest, the remarkably successful Bute-shire Natural History Society, which was founded in 1905 as successor to the Archaeological and Physical Society of Bute, an organisation dating back to 1872. In the span of nearly 70

years since its inauguration, Buteshire Natural History Society
has made a major contribution not only to the life of the
community but to the study and body of knowledge relating
to physical aspects of the island.

Achievements in archaeology have been impressive, and both
practical excavations, and the distinguished studies based on
them, have attracted attention and received justified praise
from beyond the island. The aim of promoting interest in all
aspects of the environment has been fully maintained, and the
Society, with a present membership of about 150, continues to
thrive. Apart from its notable contribution to archaeology,
the study of geology, geography, botany, ornithology, and
meteorology has been pursued, and local research has provided
valuable new knowledge. The Society maintains the Bute
Natural History museum and associated library in Rothesay,
and publishes its important papers in bound volumes under
the title of *Transactions of the Buteshire Natural History Society*,
which in 1970 reached its eighteenth volume after 60 years of
publication. The society has its own photographic section, and
an associated group of Bute Junior Naturalists under Miss
Dorothy Marshall.

Another successful local club is the North Bute Literary
Society, whose weekly meetings are held in Port Bannatyne
where the society is based, though in some respects it is the
successor to the Rothesay Literary Association, which was
prominent in the last decades of the nineteenth century. One
of the subjects for a meeting in 1879 was a debate under the
title 'Ought Manhood Suffrage to be Universal?' According to
the local newspaper report of the debate 'a majority voted for
the negative'.

Rothesay Business Club is prominent among the many
other thriving societies, while the Rotary Club of Rothesay,
in addition to its regular meetings and activities, has sponsored
two large and successful exhibitions in recent years, the first
featuring Careers and Hobbies and the second Hobbies and

Page 143 (*above*) The Rhubodach Car Ferry which plies across the narrow Kyles of Bute to the mainland; (*below*) Wemyss Bay–Rothesay car ferry: the *Bute* is at present the regular connection between mainland and island for vehicles and passengers

Page 144 Rothesay in and out of season: (*above*) the new pier terminal was built in 1968 to offer modern facilities for tourists, motorists, and yachtsmen; (*below*) under snow: Bute's mild climate makes snow scenes relatively rare, but on occasion Rothesay's palm trees feature in a white winter setting

Handicrafts. An association of Rothesay Academicals caters for the varying interests of the Academy's former pupils.

There are several well supported amateur dramatic clubs, which present their own productions and also participate in the annual Drama Festival. A strong musical tradition is maintained by the County Musical Association, and by a number of local choirs. The Isle of Bute Country Dance Society has an enthusiastic membership, and a School of Dancing caters for devotees of Highland dancing.

There are six local institutes in the Bute Federation of the SWRI, situated at Ballianlay, Port Bannatyne, Kilchattan Bay, Craigmore, Ascog and Ardbeg, and there are also branches of the British Red Cross Society, RNLI, WRVS, and United Nations Association. Specialist interests are catered for by such organisations as the Rothesay Horticultural Society, Bute Agricultural Society, Bute Junior Agricultural Club, Rothesay and District Cage Bird Society, Isle of Bute Angling Association, Rothesay Amateur Swimming Club, and clubs for yachting, water-skiing, shinty, and football.

Rothesay Evening Institute is responsible for a varied programme of further education, while for young people there are companies of Guides, Scouts, Boys' Brigade, Sea Cadets, and a Youth Club.

The list of Bute's distinguished natives and residents is interesting, but, with one or two notable exceptions, not outstanding. Sir William MacEwen, the eminent pioneer in brain surgery, was born in Rothesay, and built a house at Garrochty at the south end of the island, where he lived for many years. A memorial has been erected at the family grave in nearby St Blane's Chapel, and a plaque marks his birthplace near the Skeoch Woods.

The celebrated post-impressionist painter, and exceptionally fine colourist of the Glasgow School, Leslie Hunter, was born in Rothesay in 1879. He left Scotland for California at the age of thirteen, and worked as an illustrator in San Francisco, where he knew the novelist Jack London. On the eve of his first one-man show as an artist, all his paintings were destroyed in the great San Francisco earthquake of 1906. Returning to Scotland he worked as an illustrator in Glasgow, continuing to develop his painting, and making frequent visits to France, where his passion for colour grew even stronger. He was greatly influenced by the work of Cezanne, and his avowed wish was to see more colour in Scottish life. His own paintings were striking contributions to that aim, and the Loch Lomond paintings are outstanding in that respect, prompting his fellow-artist Peploe to comment: 'That is Hunter at his best, and it is as fine as any Matisse'.

Leslie Hunter was largely self-taught, and with his contemporaries, Cadell and Peploe, brought a new dimension to Scottish painting. He died in 1931, and in August 1955 an impressive exhibition of his paintings, arranged by the Arts Council for Buteshire Natural History Society, was on view in his native town.

Montague Stanley, well known as an actor on the Edinburgh stage, was also a painter, and came to live for many years in Ascog, where his burial place is still referred to locally as 'the painter's grave'. A long-term resident, J. W. Mackail, had a family which included novelists Dennis Mackail and Angela Thirkell. Shorter-term residents included Captain Marryat, who wrote *Midshipman Easy* at Little Barone; and Mrs Craik, author of *John Halifax Gentleman,* and also unexpectedly composer of the oft-rendered ballad, *Rothesay Bay*:

> It's a bonnie bay at morning
> And bonnier at noon,
> And bonniest when the sun draps
> And red comes up the moon
>
> When the mist creeps o'er the Cumbraes,
> And Arran peaks are grey,
> And the great black hills, like sleeping kings
> Sit grand roun' Rothesay Bay.

John Sterling, critic and essayist, who was the subject of a Carlyle biography, was born at Kames Castle, while an unusually distinctive character, R. B. Cunninghame Graham—Scottish patriot, pioneer of modern nationalism, a celebrated traveller, and author of the minor classic *Tscheffely's Ride*—had a house at St Anne's Lodge, Ascog. He was an inveterate supporter of minority causes, and after a demonstration supporting Home Rule for Ireland he was given a prison sentence. As a member of parliament he was fearless in debate, and when on one occasion he was asked to withdraw a remark or suffer suspension, he replied firmly, 'I never withdraw'.

Over the years the island appears to have had a special attraction for actors, including Allan Wilkie, Montague Stanley, and Sheridan Knowles, who followed his famous master to Bute; but the name of that master, Edmund Kean, is the one above all that has added a fascinating interlude in the story of Bute. Kean's connection spanned only a few years, but the strange and unique episode provided an interest that still casts its spell over the island, and deserves a chapter of its own for the telling.

8 A COTTAGE ON THE ISLE OF BUTE

THE great actor Edmund Kean had temporarily lost favour with his public because of adverse publicity arising from his private behaviour, when, between acts of Richard III at Greenock, with his audience 'waiting for his overthrow at Bosworth Field', he left the theatre still dressed for his part, boarded a boat and set sail for Bute. On that occasion his house there proved a refuge, as it was to be again and again. In 1827, after playing at Cherbourg, he toured the towns along the west coast 'to reach his sanctuary at Bute', and after hectic performances, American tours, and many farewells to the theatre, he 'rested in his cottage in Bute'.

In 1822 he had planned a paradise there, and a tomb. A paradise it always was in the ten years of life left to him, but not a tomb—he was buried in Old Richmond Church in 1833, forty-six years old. In the summer of 1822 when he was on tour, he saw a cottage on the banks of Loch Fad, the Butt of Woodend, and went ahead with arrangements to buy the property from Lord Bute, through the agency of Robert Thom. In a letter to Lord Bute's factor in 1824, Robert Thom wrote:

> I have received another letter from Mr. Kean in which he expresses a desire to take the whole Butt for 99 years and leaves me to make the best terms I can with Lord Bute. Now this rather embarrasses me, for as his Lordship in the whole of this affair has evidently acted more with the view to accommodate Mr. Kean than anything else, I cannot propose any terms to his Lordship different from those he has offered. Upon looking over the ground carefully, however, I think we have been wrong

both as to its extent and value—that is, there appears to be more acres upon the whole than we supposed, but the value by the acre less. I had supposed that when two pounds per acre was asked that this was about double the value of the land to a farmer, and I stated this to Mr. Kean as very moderate considering the length of the lease. Upon going over every part of the ground yesterday, however, I incline to think that no man, however active, could pay from the land only above 12/- an acre—but at present there are no less than three separate families, and the accomodation to each of a house and garden and cows grass is what chiefly pays the present rent. I should not trouble with these statements, but that I feel myself bound to explain everything to Mr. Kean as we go on—because he has trusted everything to me, and because *I have realy been the chief cause of his fixing his residence in Bute*—Besides, however trifling the matter may appear at present, yet it has every chance to become the subject of history, and will upon the whole I think be another feather in the cap of the island. On this account I am anxious that the matter should be fully considered in all its parts, and that Mr. Kean should not only be pleased with the Island and his bargain in the mean time, but also after he has settled in the place.

To come to the point at once, I should feel no hesitation in closing for the whole Butt for 99 years at £30 a year—(because 15 acres was the quantity said to be in it when he was here, and I know he would feel disappointed if the sum were greater) but I could not go further without again consulting him.

Will you have the goodness therefore to communicate the substance of this (too long) letter to his Lordship before he leaves the Island, and favour me with his pleasure on the subject.

Lord Bute's answering note to his factor was brief: 'The land is let as accomodation land, and cannot be given for 99 years at less than forty shillings per Scottish acre, good or bad'.

In April of that year Robert Thom wrote to the factor Archibald Moore describing an attempt to plan a road to Woodend nearer the loch than the existing one, with the intention of approaching the house from the front.

I went up to Woodend yesterday between Chapleton march and Woodend House (or Kean's Cottage?) but, from the position of the house with respect to the grounds, found it impossible to carry a road to the house, in good taste through Mr. Kean's land. The reason is, that the road, lead it as you will through Woodend ground, comes direct upon the back and end of the house, and the front is never seen till you are at the door. This makes an extremely awkward approach, considering the localities of the place. I next explored all the *possibilities in the vicinity* to see if a better approach could anywhere else be found —but none presented itself except we were to lead the road through the planting between Woodend and Loch Fad. Upon examining this line I found a most delightful walk could be made through this planting, beginning nearly at Chapleton march and coming out near the shore of Loch Fad, just below the front of the house. That you may the more easily understand what I mean I send enclosed a plan or rather sketch of the whole which I made without injuring the planting and found that, in my opinion, it could. By care in forming such a path it may be led in such a way as not to interfere with a tree of any note, and you are aware that when a planting is grown up like it the breadthe of a road of 10 or 12 feet is less than the distance that ought to be between any two trees. That is you would not have a tree taken out by the road which ought to stand.

From his sketch it can be seen that the present road follows the road that led from the old farm cottages, extending to Woodend and still coming on the house from the back. Thom was an excellent representative for the actor and carried the sale of Woodend through successfully at a rent of £48 per year. In his letters to the factor, Thom was always careful to point out the character of his client.

Only I know Mr. Kean is extremely sensitive, and easily irritated at any thing which he may consider in the light of binding him too tight and you know he is not a business man— but really acts in the impulse of feeling or temper, rather than the result of calm deliberation and I really have had more to do to manage him on this account, than you are aware of.

He must have known how much the idea of the island home that 'all the monarchs of the world might envy' meant to Kean.

In 1824 the new tenant of Woodend settled with his wife and son for the autumn, made improvements, planted a mulberry tree, and selected a spot where he declared he would make a vault for the reception of his remains.

He had been the great genius of the stage of his time, playing to packed houses at Drury Lane and in provincial theatres. Coleridge had said of him, 'Seeing him act was like reading Shakespeare by flashes of lightning', and Hazlitt, who gave enthusiastic criticisms of all his great roles, thought his Othello 'the finest piece of acting in the world'. The French actor Talma had given a banquet for him in Paris, where members of the Theatre Français had presented him with a gold snuffbox, and he had been feted everywhere with presentations and public dinners. Already there were cracks in the marvellous façade of his stupendous success. His affair with Mrs Cox was to lead to the notorious Cox trial in January 1825, and with that, part of his public grew hostile to him. As Alderman Cox sued him for £2,000 as 'compensation for loss of the affection and company of his wife', it cost him heavily, too. The payment for his performances at £50 a night increased to catch up with his debts. He had known illness, was drinking heavily, and was subject to fits of depression. The nervous energy required to sustain his output of 'star' Shakespearian roles must have been enormous. After his flight from Richard III at Greenock, he played in Manchester and Dublin, and by June was back in London. In July he had finished this series of performances and was preparing for his second American tour (the first in 1820, had been a fantastic success).

The theatre, which had been his inspiration, where he said he became alive, a whole person, was becoming part of the wheel of material necessity that was to crush him. The dreams he had invested in his cottage in Bute, his feeling of nostalgia for a more perfect life, always haunted him. Just before he left for the American tour his friend Grattan gave a poignant account of Kean singing 'Lord Ullin's Daughter'. Tom Moore's songs were also great favourites with Kean, and, listening to him, Grattan felt the gentleness and sadness of the man that were lost somewhere in the celebrity. Public condemnation of his private life followed him to America, where his audiences gave him many violent receptions. 'Like a howl of wolves' was the reaction of his Boston audience, but his acting won the day, and by the end of the tour he was favourably received, and of course welcomed back with great acclaim at Drury Lane. It is strange to think that the public who censored his drinking and dissolution were affecting his private life even more seriously. Not only was he taken ill in New York, but on a visit to an asylum there, while studying the madness of Lear, he made an attempt on his own life: 'I'll walk to the ridge of the roof and make a leap, it is the best end I can make of my life'.

In a way Bute was his hope, his idyll, for he kept a vision of the perfect family life even months before the Cox trial. There was never a chance for his wife at Woodend. She suspected her husband of burying her in the country.

> He took 22 acres of land from Lord Bute's Factor—Lord Bute's property—as sterile—as damp—as forlorn—as desolate as you can conceive—built and furnished a House in a spot where there was no road or any creature within three miles of the place—he paid two pound an acre for what was not worth five shillings—and now no one will purchase it, even the factor from whom it was purchased refused to give three hundred for the House—it was a madness done by the desire of Mrs. Cox to hide me in and ended in utter ruin to us all died without a shilling everything sold for a quarter its value not one shilling for his wife and son he had to climb a steep Hill to gain a livelihood.

This letter, written after her husband's death, is bitter. Mary Kean had been separated from her husband for years, but he had continued to support her financially during his life. Their son Charles had been educated at Eton before going on the stage, against his father's wishes. Kean had very selfishly declared that he would be 'the first and last actor of his name'. His own account of finances is just as biased as his wife's but from the opposite point of view. 'When I last visited America the whole of my possessions on arrival was twenty pounds, leaving her my house on Bute (which all the monarchs of the world might envy) and £600 per year. I had scarcely recovered myself in that distant country—but I received an English paper wherein she had inserted that I had left her pennyless—to starve, in a miserable hovel in the bleak desolate Highlands of Scotland.' If Mary Kean had decided not to like the house on Bute, Edmund Kean remained faithful to his original conception of 'the most beautiful place in the world', and was always proud of the house that he had planned in such a setting. He delighted, too, in the idea of a literary retreat, where friends, sharing his interest in the theatre, could meet and talk. He wrote to fellow actor Charles Kemble, 'Shakespeare you and I, would form most excellent companionship', and the four busts at his gates of Shakespeare, Massinger, Garrick and Kean are the first impression that a visitor has of Woodend. As a contrast to husband and wife's highly subjective reports, we have a clear-eyed account written in a letter from Mary Kean's sister, Susan Chambers, to a friend in Waterford in 1824. Susan had accompanied the Keans to help with the removal, and gives an excellent description of the journey north and the voyage down the Clyde to Rothesay.

Glasgow is a very handsome large and well built city—but tho a week in it owing to constant wet weather—which Scotland is famed for, I could not see it to advantage. On Friday we got in to the steam boat for Bute and tho fine setting off, it poured as tho it were its last—before we got half way down the Clyde—that being too flat on either side, and the river narrow; we passed Dunbarton Castle which Wallace took, Port Glasgow, Greenock and other places to take in as well as let out passengers, and were five hours in coming to Rothesay, which is the best town on this Island, the bay belonging to it is really the most beautiful I ever saw or could have had a conception of—it is small and surrounded with most magnificent mountains—each vying with its neighbour in beauty and grandeur—the town is extremely ugly—and small but it is greatly resorted to by the people of Glasgow as a sea bathing place.

Of Woodend she says:

To say it is beautiful is not in my mind saying half enough—it is in fact perfectly enchanting but so lonely—one almost startles at the sound of their own voice, but its loneliness is no imperfection to me—indeed it gives me the idea that all nature was in repose—so very sweet and tranquil is all round. My sister would not speak of it in this manner—she never did—and I fear never will like it. I am sorry for it tho I cannot blame her—it surely is preposterous to think a man gay as he is will always be content to remain here—and without him Mary ought not. It has occasioned her many bitter tears, but I try all I can to engage her in improving and decorating it. She does it but with a heavy heart. The house stands in a pretty little lawn—about 60 feet from a lake which is two miles and a half long and in winter very wide. The ground slopes up which ends in a high hill richly wooded and in summer enameled with flowers; this hill is at the back of the Building which looks towards the lake and consists of a pretty stone vestibule and Hall, stone staircase, on one side is a very good dining room, doors of communication to Edmund's library—which is about four times the size of his London one—the windows of the whole are down to the ground—on the other side is a very pretty bedchamber in which I sleep—next to it is a large kitchen, a water closet in the hall, a large landing place leads you on one side to a drawing room 30 feet by 20 and high in proportion, one window looks to the woody hill another to the lake and a third takes in the whole compass of the ground which is about 36 acres, mostly indeed consisting of barren rocks, with swamps interspersed but all picturesque. On the other side of the landing place there are two excellent bedchambers, the one in front is my sister's, the back Charles's. Mary's room has a beautiful little dressing room attached to it with one door opening into the drawing the other into her room—the whole of these appartments are beautifully furnished and when papered and painted (which is to be done while they are in London) will be truly magnificent. To this building which certainly would be too small, Mary has added a couple of wings—one on either side the one next the Kitchen has Nellie's bedchamber, a wash house, coal cellar and larder in it, that on the other has two bedchambers—a dairy and wine cellar, so you see it is no cottage but a good chunk of a thick set stone building, that looks to living many hundred years. There is a man engaged for has 1s. 6d. per day per man; now it is two pence less—so you see what an expence he is at, tho he thought when he took it that we could live for nothing—meat is as dear as in London only the weight is larger—bread the same, fish is not very good—that is—it mostly consists of whiting and haddock—we have liberty to fish in the lake and to shoot or course. Edmund when here went out twice and got two hares each time; he was but a fortnight at home. When the wings are finished I shall take one of the rooms and leave my present room for any visitor—when Edmund returns he is to bring a low four wheeled carriage—such as I can drive in his absence. I am to buy a cow in the spring—when we shall have cream and butter of our own, but before we can drive any carriage here we must at least lay out a hundred pound to form a road, for at present there is nothing but a foot path. I daresay you have heard of all the trouble he has involved himself in through that wretched Mrs. Cox—how it will end heaven only knows. I believe he will go to America after his London engagements this winter.

There is a nice little testimonial to the character of the inhabitants of the island in the postscript. 'When you write pray tell me all the news. I have got a little parrot to keep me company which Edmund sent me and two dogs—tho the people are so honest there is no need of them.'

By 1828 Kean's affairs on Bute were being looked after in his absence by a Mr Corkindale, landlord of the *Bute Arms*. There is a letter to him, written in March of that year:

Dear Corkindale,
    The multiplicity of business I am at present engaged in prevented me from answering your letter on the instant. It was my hope to have visited the Isle of Bute at the termination of my engagement at the Theatre Covent Garden, which takes place

March 30th, but I find it impractable. My engagements are numerous and must be fulfilled. On my return from France, which will be about the end of June, I shall repair to the happy Isle as fast as horses and steam boat can carry me. You will oblige me therefore by acting as my agent during the interval of absence, and direct Reed to let me find the grounds on my return precisely as I have been accustomed to see them. I do not understand gardening technicalities, but they always looked very beautiful and beautiful I wish them to remain.

My health is very fast improving and the public favors greatly increasing and yet I do not know how it is, amidst the blaze of popularity that is the natural attendant upon the favorites of caprice, I cannot help envying the poorest peasant that doffs his cap to the visitor of Rothesay—however if the world and my profession prevents me living there it remains with myself the power of dying there, and even that, I look forward to with gratification . . . you will do me a favor, if you will enquire of the housekeeper and Reed whether or not I am in arrears. If so, be kind enough to pay them, and I will send you the amount by return of Post. Direct form, as usual Theatre Royal, Covent Garden and entre nous, if I had known Mrs. Clarke had been inclined to bring dirty children with her, I should have invoked the shades of Herod before they had polluted my Temple

Yours very truly,
Edmund Kean

We are told that Kean liked to stop at the gatehouse for a welcoming glass on his return visits before his carriage rolled up the drive to his home. John Reid was gardener at Woodend and his daughter remembered those occasions very well: 'I min' Kean liked a wee drap and always came into the lodge for it every time he passed out or in the gate. He had a press there to keep it in, but he would never take it unless my mother was there to give it to him'. As an old woman she remembered how Edmund gave her a pony so that she could ride in and out of Rothesay by herself—and once tickets for *Richard III* in Glasgow. She had not recognised him in his make-up and when she told Edmund that 'Richard was a very ugly man', he had laughed. 'Ah', she said. 'Kean was a very kind man and very

156

charitable to all around him.' Another child on the Woodend estate was Sandy Nisbet, and, like John Reid's daughter, he lived to his eighties with happy memories of Edmund Kean, of his kindness to children, although 'he had little regard for the Sabbath staying in bed till late afternoon and then went fishing on the loch'.

Bute was Kean's headquarters in the summer of 1828. Charles Kean visited him then, but did not stay at Woodend House, as by that time Mary Kean had separated from her husband. The son chose instead to lodge with the Reids in the cottage by the gates, but he was reconciled with his father and played with him in Glasgow in October in a performance of Howard Payne's *Brutus*. During this period Kean's acting was spasmodic, since drinking and illness had made his memory unreliable. In 1829 he was 'obliged to retire to his cottage in Bute', and spent his birthday there, but in the company of an unprincipled woman known as 'Ophelia', which did not help his general condition; and there were to be breakdowns on the stage and angry confrontations with his audiences ahead. He always faced up to his public.

'What do you want?'
'You, you, you.'
'Well then here I am. I have acted in every theatre in the United Kingdom of Great Britain and Ireland, and in all the principal towns throughout the U.S.A. but in my life I have never acted to such a set of ignorant brutes as I now see before me.'

Such a spirit was to keep him going throughout another London season, playing Richard III, Shylock (the part that had first made him famous in 1814), Sir Giles Overreach, and King Lear. In July 1830 the King's Theatre was packed to suffocation for a farewell benefit before his departure for New York, but he was not able to make the journey because of illness and again rested in his cottage in Bute. He applied to become a lessee of the Richmond Theatre, and bought a house in Richmond. In March 1833 he appeared at Covent Garden as Othello with Charles as Iago. When he came to the lines

> O! now, for ever
> Farewell the tranquil mind; farewell content!
> Farewell! Othello's occupation's gone

there was stormy applause from the audience. Kean stood motionless and fixed, his chin resting on his breast, his eyes riveted to the ground. The audience fell silent. He was partially roused to consciousness of the scene, looked round him, advanced a few steps towards Iago, who said, 'Is it possible my lord?' Othello's words were 'Villain, be-sure-you-prove—' and suddenly Kean flung himself on his son: 'Oh God, I am dying. Speak to them Charles'. Surely his last stage performance was his most dramatic. That was in March. Before he died in May 1833, he wrote to his wife,

> My dear Mary,
>   Let us be no longer fools. Come home; forget and forgive. If I have erred, it was in my head not my heart, and most severely have I suffered for it. My future life shall be employed in contributing to your happiness; and you, I trust, will return that feeling by a total obliteration of the past.
> Your wild but really affectionate husband,
Edmund Kean

His creditors were waiting for him. Only a few days before his death he was in danger of being arrested for a debt of £100. After his death they seized on all his possessions, presents, his cottage in Bute, and his house at Richmond where he died and was buried.

The notices of the sale of Woodend are flamboyant indeed, and read like playbills of the time. A different estimate of the property was given to the Marquess by his factor John Muir:

> It's my candid view that I have estimated both the value and supposed return too high altho I have made every allowance for the name and character of the person to whom it belonged, but however far that might go in England, I am convinced much

value will not be attached to it in Scotland and the place will only sell or let according to the comfort, beauty or accomodation which it may be supposed to afford. The House is very defficient in many respects and would require painting of which it stands in much need. Additional accomodation to render it at all comfortable to a respectable family. Lands little or in no respect altered from the state in which Mr. Kean found them and nothing done to improve them beyond a small patch of garden, shrubbery etc. and to improve and lay off the lands to form a gentleman's place would cost a large sum. Thinks it proper to state these things in support of opinion differing so widely from Mr. Kean's administrators as to value of property.

As early as June 1833 Lord Bute had written to his factor:

I am inclined to purchase Kean's villa in Bute so that I may transfer it to a friend or in other words to prevent its falling into the hands of any person whom I may not approve.

Fortunately Lord Bute did buy the property and Kean's cottage has been protected with the rest of the estate. In a strange way the paradise that captured Kean's imagination has remained. Now, seen across the loch on a golden September morning, surrounded by quiet hills and woods, the charm of Woodend seems flawless. Intriguing that a passionate actor yearned for this serenity, and yet small wonder that his instinct for Shakespeare's great roles could recognise it; and the house, as Susan Chambers described it, with its lovely curved staircase and windows looking to Loch Fad, is still Kean's cottage.

9   *THE HOLIDAY ISLE*

FOR a century and a half the Firth of Clyde has been a holiday centre, particularly for the citizens of Glasgow and surrounding industrial districts. The bays, islands, and sea-lochs of the Firth, with sheltered waters and sheltering hills, have exerted a tremendous appeal over those million inhabitants who not only came to the various towns and villages along the shore for brief periods of rest and recuperation, but adopted the places of the Clyde almost as an annexe of Glasgow, investing their favourite haunt with their own particular atmosphere. Thus the rival attractions of Rothesay or Dunoon, Millport or Brodick, Innellan or Tighnabruaich, could be eagerly supported or contested by the dwellers of Partick or Govan, Pollockshields or Kelvinside. Perhaps the island of Bute was more subject to this holiday enthusiasm than anywhere else, and Rothesay became for a time each summer, if not exactly Glasgow-by-the-sea, at least an extended part of that city's legend.

Yet in acknowledging this, it must also be remembered that Bute has attracted large numbers of holiday visitors from much farther afield, and English visitors in particular have possibly been even more appreciative of the scenic attractions of places like the Kyles of Bute. For many summers it could be said that outside the traditional Glasgow, Greenock, and Paisley holiday periods, southern accents were in the ascendancy on the piers and promenades.

The holiday visitor is vital to the economy of Bute, but the obvious danger in the development of tourism as a main industry is the changing leisure patterns and fashions from

160

generation to generation. Bute has been surprisingly resistant to change over the past 100 years, and although some complain that there has been a lack of enterprise in developing Rothesay as a modern holiday resort, its appeal has survived remarkably well. Obviously concessions have had to be made to the different pattern of holidays, particularly in the matters of transport and accommodation.

Surprisingly the problems, the doubts, and the worries, have scarcely changed at all in a century, as the following extract from the *Buteman* of 14 June 1879 indicates:

> We need not expect that this summer will be characterised by the same bustle and activity to which we were accustomed in former years. We may have a busy season but it will be a short season. The demand for houses for July and August is good though principally confined to larger classes of house. Houses of one or two rooms and kitchen are scarcely asked for, indicative that the working man feels the effect of dull trade. Some people are under the impression that the country will never emerge from the present state of depression.

There is a familiar ring about that old cutting which suggests that even then the old days seemed best; obviously the recurring problems and complaints of shortness of season, the effect of poor trade and industrial conditions, and similar situations bearing on tourism, are no new features. Always there were worries about depression and decline.

THE DEVELOPING RESORT

The earliest history of Bute's emergence as a watering-place is suggested in old council minutes and newspaper advertisements. The following announcement appeared in the advertising columns of the *Glasgow Mercury* in 1786:

> Salt water quarter to let. At the point of Towart, opposite to the old kirk, two rooms and a kitchen, furnished. Most conveniently situated for sea bathing. Great variety of fish to be got

near the house, and a regular communication by the Rothesay post-boat, three times a week—Apply to John Hair at the old kirk.

It became fashionable for the tobacco lords and prosperous merchants of Glasgow to take up summer residence out of the city, and acquire a house and yacht along the shores of the Firth of Clyde. Bute's favourite places for the wealthy citizens were Craigmore, Ascog, and Montford, with Ardbeg on the other shore of the bay just that little lower on the social scale. Some of the larger houses built around that time are still in existence, but now used as boarding houses, convalescent homes, and residential schools.

As the century proceeded Rothesay's reputation as a holiday resort grew, and extravagant claims began to be made. A magazine article of 1840 stated that 'the air of Rothesay is remarkably mild and genial which has led many to call the place the Montpelier of Scotland'. Other writers compared Rothesay Bay favourably with the Bay of Naples, and it was frequently referred to as the Naples of the north, or as Scotland's Madeira.

In later Victorian times the holiday habit spread down the social scale—with the smaller red-sandstone villas that began to extend in both directions along the front to Ardbeg and Craigmore, catering for the middle class, while the tenements of the old town specialised in working-class visitors. On both levels the elaborate summer fortnight 'flittings' of luggage, bedding, prams, etc, became a familiar sight on the boats and at the piers.

The foreshore was opened up for holidaymakers, a new esplanade was built, the coastal road widened, and a bathing station established at the west bay. Around the same period the hotel and boarding-house tourist trade developed, and there was a sizeable increase in the number of day trippers.

The great days of Bute's prominence as a holiday resort were during the period between 1880 and 1910. Not only was steamer traffic at its height, and the number of holiday visitors at a record level, but there were all kinds of imaginative ideas in entertainment, and varied opportunities of excursions and activities. During this spell Glasgow's legendary pilgrimage 'doon the watter' was built up, and Rothesay's popularity reached its peak.

An idea of the varied attractions can be had from a study of newspapers, advertisements, and tourist literature of the time. The *Clyde Programme* for 1896–7 lists the different steamer cruises, concerts, band performances, and variety entertainments, available. Typical accommodation advertisements included:

> Rothesay—Attic flat 2 stairs up, 5 apartment, splendid view, month of August £6.
> Bute—The Hermitage, Ascog. House to let furnished. £20 monthly.

At the turn of the century George Eyre-Todd enthused over the attractions of Rothesay as a holiday resort. In a typically idyllic passage quoted in Maurice Lindsay's *The Lowlands of Scotland* he wrote:

> The town and bay all summer long make up a brilliant scene. There are steamers constantly coming in from the outer world with crowds of gay and happy folk, then going off, with dusky plumes of smoke and dazzling tracks of foam, across the blue waters that wind into the far recesses of the hills. There are yachts that come sweeping with white wings silently round cape and inlet. And there are the little boats that dance everywhere merrily on the sparkling sea.

Novelist Neil Munro was also a staunch Firth of Clyde man, but perhaps less enthusiastic and more balanced in his assessment of the situation when he wrote in 1907:

> It is perhaps the stranger's only fault with the Firth of Clyde that Glasgow has so palpably usurped it. He finds the shores interminably fringed by villas that have 'suburb' written large on every feature.

But the Glasgow influence certainly helped trade while the holiday boom lasted, and although there were slight signs of slackening in the last seasons before World War I, there was no evidence of pessimism. A newspaper report of 21 June 1912 anticipated an excellent season, with new holiday attractions and still more new steamers to add to the already impressive holiday fleet:

> Popular sailings started for the season last night, when the fine new steamer *Queen Empress* carried a goodly company to Glen Sannox, Arran, via Largs and Millport... Music for those wishing to dance was provided by the Excelsior String Band.

Those last prewar summers still survive in the minds of the very old as golden days that might have lasted for ever, but the reality is somewhat different. Holiday fashions were already changing, and even the wonderful Clyde sailing programme had passed its high-water mark and was on the ebb. The advent of the war merely intensified and dramatised the trend.

After the enforced lull of the years between 1914 and 1918 Bute emerged again as a holiday centre, at first on a subdued scale; but in the early 1920s there was a temporary resurgence, which aroused hopes of a complete revival of past glories. The little steamers, or at least those of them that had survived war service as minesweepers and auxiliary naval vessels, began to sail again with full colours flying. Even the large-scale yacht regattas were revived, and in 1920 a visit from King George V brought out the old 'royal regatta' headlines, and raised hopes that the brave days of Clyde glory had returned.

However, at best this was merely an afterglow. For a time the great yachts returned, with Sir Thomas Lipton and his successive *Shamrocks* attracting large crowds to witness renewals of earlier attempts to win the America's Cup. New steamers were built to replace the old, and once again evening cruises, musical cruises, fireworks, and illumination displays, supplemented the natural attractions of sailing in Clyde waters. The

Glasgow Fair crowds still flocked to Rothesay, and day trippers became even more numerous—but recession was on the way.

Various factors contributed to the eventual decline: notably the slump and unemployment of the 1930s, the increase of foreign travel, the gradual reduction of the steamer fleet, and the rival holiday attractions of English resorts, offering more modern entertainment. Nevertheless in the two decades between the wars Bute remained an important holiday centre, and Rothesay and the Firth of Clyde retained the persistent allegiance and sentimental loyalty of the generations who had known it in its great days, and others who instinctively felt it was part of the local folklore.

World War II had a more traumatic effect. It would be true to say that 1939, that last glorious summer of apparently endless warm days and calm seas, and even an international regatta, was a swansong. After this war the earlier glory of Bute as a holiday island, and Rothesay as a resort, was never fully recaptured. Foreign travel provided serious rival attractions to all classes of holidaymakers, and it was difficult to project exciting counter appeal with a depleted sailing fleet and decaying holiday attractions. Something of the legend had died also, and although attempts to set up a rival 'Costa Clyde' image were made, it became obvious that Bute must complete on a different level for the attention of holidaymakers.

The scale and scope are different, but there is some evidence that Bute is adapting its resources to cater for the modern tourist—widening the catchment area, exploiting its unique appeal as a small island, and, reluctantly perhaps, thinking in terms of car-ferries for motorists instead of gaily coloured steamers for cruises through the Kyles. And despite the difficulties, there is cautious optimism that the island can maintain its tourist importance in a new age.

The natural advantages of the island as a holiday centre are indisputable; in a comparatively small area there is a remarkable variety of scenery. Within a few miles of Rothesay there are several attractive bays and sandy beaches; yet, on the other hand, only a mile or two farther north lies an area of wild hill and moorland country, where the walker can wander all day without meeting a soul.

Bute has many unspoiled regions where a rich variety of bird and plant life can be observed. The extent and diversity of birds is exceptional. The island is well watered, with a number of delightful lochs, and there is pleasant woodland. The presence of interesting geological and geographical features enhances the interest, while there is an abundance of archaeological and historical relics. In fact the sense of an unbroken chain of history, the presence of continuous human life from the most remote past to the busy present, is the island's chief enchantment.

A main attraction is the number of superb and extensive views. The vantage point of Canada Hill provides a panorama covering much of the Firth of Clyde, the Argyll and Cowal hills, and a distant view of several counties. The name Canada Hill arose from the fact that relatives of those who sailed to Canada on emigrant ships could take a last look at the boats as they sailed slowly but relentlessly on the long stretch between the Cloch, Cumbraes, and Arran, on the way to exile across the seas.

From the other side of the hill the view northwards to the lochs and hills of Argyll is even more impressive, while the closer view of Arran's mountains, and the prominent Sleeping Warrior, is also outstanding. On a lower height the view of Glen Sannox across the water from Dunagoil is as effective as any.

166

Bute is ideal for walking, cycling, or short-distance driving. The walks by the old moor-roads or on the hills and shores are especially interesting, while the roads are well surfaced and in the main relatively quiet.

The Buteshire Natural History Society publishes an excellent series of Nature Trails, which suggest tours in various parts of the island and give details of points of interest on the various routes. Bute Newspapers publish a most useful pamphlet, *Walks and Drives in Bute*. Of the places of interest visited by tourists Rothesay Castle, St Blane's Church, Canada Hill, Dunagoil, Loch Fad, Ettrick Bay, Scalpsie Bay, Kerrycroy, Kilchattan, Ascog, Barone Hill, and Rhubodach Ferry are among the most popular.

SPORT AND RECREATIONAL FACILITIES

There are three golf courses on the island, with pride of place going to Rothesay's eighteen-hole Municipal course, which, apart from its famous views, is recognised as one of the best holiday courses in the country, and has the distinction of being designed by James Braid. Port Bannatyne has the unlikely attraction of a thirteen-hole course, five holes being played twice to make up the full round, while Kingarth is a pleasant nine-hole seaside course. Putting on Rothesay Esplanade attracts more customers than any other outdoor pastime. Bute has four well kept bowling greens at Ardbeg, Ballochgoy, Craigmore, and Kingarth, and there are six tennis courts at Rothesay's Meadows.

Swimmers are catered for by the modern indoor heated seawater pool at Battery Place, which is regarded as the finest of its kind in the West of Scotland. Galas takes place during the season, and there is a comfortable spectating balcony. Remedial and sauna baths are available. The days of the great yachting regattas may have passed, but Rothesay and Port Bannatyne Bays can still be packed with summer craft. Yacht races remain a part of the Clyde scene, and the Isle of Bute Sailing Club organises dinghy races and an open regatta. Boating is a popular summer pastime, with sea-angling trips very much in demand, while motorboat cruises to the Kyles of Bute, Loch Striven, and Kerrycroy attract many.

Although the steamer sailing programme may seem meagre compared with the enterprise of the past, there is still in high summer a remarkably varied choice of cruises. Inveraray, Arran, Cumbrae, Campbeltown, Tighnabruaich, and Loch Long, are favourite destinations, but there are other shorter trips to mainland piers. Cruising on Clyde waters must remain a unique holiday attraction.

Despite the restricted distances, coach tours on the island are popular, and some are extended by use of ferry, or combined sea and road excursions. Bute's accessibility, with a choice of three routes by train and boat, and two by road and ferry, is an advantage to holidaymakers.

Most of the varied amenities of a holiday centre are available in Rothesay and district. The town itself has over 100 hotels and boarding houses, and the tourist accommodation is officially listed as extending to over 2,000 beds for visitors, to say nothing of extensive private-house letting, the range varying from a 120 bedroom five-star hotel to rooms with attendance in small houses. Even this large-scale provision can be taxed when the normal winter population of 7,000 is increased to a midsummer peak of over 30,000. In 1955 nearly 140,000 visitors were accommodated in hotels and boarding houses, and over 700,000 visitors landed at Rothesay pier (more than half of them in July and August). Although there was a decrease in numbers during the 1960s, the figures remain impressive, while the ever-increasing total of landings from the car ferries compensates to some extent for the depleted passenger steamer service. An efficient and forward-looking publicity organisation, sponsored by Rothesay Advertising Association, is responsible for the running of an Information Bureau at the pier. During the past

168

15 years, under the direction of Mr J. A. Duguid, this office has dealt with many thousands of applications for accommodation and information on matters of local interest.

Lack of entertainment is sometimes a complaint directed against Rothesay, and possibly the town has not been over-successful in adapting to the changing needs. This was not always the case, for in the past some of Rothesay's traditional entertainments had a fame beyond the island, especially the variety shows at the Winter Gardens. The Rothesay Entertainers became famous not only as a part of local and visiting Glasgow life but also as a fertile training ground for comedians and singers. Jack Anthony, Dave Willis, Renee Houston, Tommy Morgan, Alec Finlay, and Dickie Henderson, figure among the famous names, but perhaps the most renowned from a purely local point of view was Charlie Kemble, whose spontaneous rhyming and exploiting of audience participation made him a popular favourite year after year. It is difficult to describe or analyse the peculiar mixture of ingredients that made for the tremendous appeal of those entertainers, but the memory is of Scots kitchen comedy at its broadest, interspersed with song scenas and a dash of local and tartan colour. Now the era has passed, and the shows are usually a pale imitation of former glories, although occasionally the top stars of Scottish entertainment, for instance the Corries, come to the old concrete-floored umbrella-roofed hall, and bring the crowds back again.

The Pavilion, a modern multi-purpose centre, was built in 1937, and remains the town's foremost hall for concerts, dances, and entertainments. Rothesay had four cinemas for a time— the Regal, the Ritz, the Palace, and the De Luxe—but even the sole survivor, the Regal, is now forced to alternate film shows with the inevitable Bingo. Apart from the regular attractions, special events are held during the season, and among the highlights are the traditional Rothesay Fair in July and Bute Highland Games in August.

THE FUTURE

Bute is aware of the need to adapt its resources to meet the demands of modern tourism. Already the motorist is being given improved services and facilities, and efforts are being made to win a share of the 'second holiday' market, by offering off-season package holidays. In 1968 a report entitled *A Study of Tourism in the Firth of Clyde* was published by the Scottish Tourist Board as Phase 1 of the Firth of Clyde study, while in the same year Bute County Council published a report on Development and Tourism. Among the proposals were plans to encourage foreign tourists, stressing the importance of providing superior accommodation.

In general the future of Bute as a holiday resort seems assured, but the precise pattern of development has not yet been determined. On a long-term view it is essential that, whatever the plans, the superb natural attractions of a small island should be preserved.

10   THE STEAMERS & THE
FIRTH OF CLYDE

BUTE has always been a natural sailing centre, and Rothesay a vital link in the unique Firth of Clyde steamer service, which covers almost 1,200 square miles of sheltered coastal waters, around islands, long sea-lochs, and shore scenery unsurpassed in the British Isles. The saga of these little ships is full of excitement, colour, and gaiety, and their history over a century and a half is closely connected with the island's development.

With the introduction of steamships in the early years of the nineteenth century, the passenger service between Glasgow and the Firth of Clyde towns, which previously had been spasmodic, suddenly expanded into a flourishing trade. For the greater part of the century Glasgow's Broomielaw was the terminus for most of the Firth of Clyde sailings. All the early boats were privately owned, and it was not until the 1880s, when private enterprise began to give way to public ownership, that this all-the-way traffic was seriously challenged by companies plying from lower Clyde railway piers at Wemyss Bay, Gourock, Fairlie, Greenock, and Craigendoran.

In the middle 1830s over thirty steamers were sailing down the water from Glasgow's harbour, covering the voyage to the Tail of the Bank in about 2hr. Bute Steam Packet Company, with the *Isle of Bute* and *Maid of Bute*, were fairly early on the scene, and by the 1860s competition between the different boats was increasing, and the first of a long line of famous Clyde races between rival ships was recorded.

On 27 May 1861 one exciting contest, which has become a

legendary part of Clyde Steamer lore, involved the *Ruby* and the *Rothesay Castle*. The two ships left Glasgow for Greenock and Rothesay at 4 o'clock, and reached Greenock in 1hr 25min. After a prolonged tussle the *Rothesay Castle* triumphed by 2½min, completing the Glasgow–Rothesay trip in the record time of 2hr 28min.

The aftermath of this struggle took place in court, when the rival skippers were charged with reckless navigation, Captain Brown of the *Rothesay Castle* being fined a guinea, and Captain Price of the *Ruby* double that amount. A possible reason for the apparent discrimination between winner and loser may have been the previous record of the latter, who had gained something of a reputation for 'dangerous driving'. Andrew McQueen, a well known Clyde steamer historian, has described several of Captain Price's exploits, including an encounter between his *Ruby* and the *Neptune*, in which the rival ships not only collided twice in the heat of the struggle, but missed out a scheduled call at Gourock pier in their efforts to reach Rothesay first.

The missing of piers, or alternatively the rapid lifting of gangways before intending passengers had a chance to embark, seemed to be an essential part of the rivalry, and the skippers were obviously ready to go to dangerous extremes in the quest for victory. It was hardly surprising when the editor of the *Glasgow Herald* issued a public rebuke to the captain of the *Ruby*:

> What right has this man Price to entrap people into his vessel for a safe summer-day sail and then subject them to the terror of a violent death by explosion or collision?

Perhaps it was inevitable that Captain Price should eventually lose his command because of continued racing exploits, but many must have a lingering admiration for a colourful character of the racing days, and perhaps a nostalgic regret for times more stirring than the present, when, as Maurice Lindsay points out 'there are no Clyde races now because there are hardly enough steamers left for two ever to be sailing in the same direction at once'.

Around this time developments down river, at Greenock on the south bank and Helensburgh on the north bank, pointed to later trends. Two newly built paddle steamers, *Dandy Dinmont* and *Meg Merrilees*, started a service from Helensburgh to Rothesay and the Kyles of Bute. Yet despite the earlier railway boom, during which rail-steamer link points had been initiated, the supremacy of the 'railway boats' was not established until nearly the closing years of the century. Some intimation of approaching rivalry was given in a news item from the *Buteman* of 1 March 1879:

STEAMBOAT SAILINGS

Communication with Glasgow by steamer direct will be more frequent on and after the 10th inst. when the *Sultan* will resume sailing for Rothesay at the convenient hour of 8.40. By the *Sultan* and the *Athole* we will now have two departures and arrivals daily in addition to the *Mountaineer* and Wemyss Bay service.

Even then the spectacular increase of Rothesay traffic to over 100 calls a day at the pier in less than 20 years could scarcely have been foreseen.

THE GOLDEN DAYS

The golden era of the Clyde steamers covered the quarter of a century between 1890 and the outbreak of World War I. During this period of tremendous activity, in memory at least, summer suns were always shining, the waters of the Clyde were alive with ships, the piers were constantly busy, the boats ablaze with colour, and the whole world was happy—or at least that part of it which sailed down the Clyde. That was the period of most of the lore—of rivalries and races, of colour and character, of record times and celebrated captains, of music and magic, of famous ships and well loved piers—that gave birth to the golden legend of the Clyde, which despite all the changes has not yet died.

The surprising thing is that the facts in most instances match

173

and confirm even the most colourful recollections! During those years there were never less than forty steamers plying on the Firth, in contrast to the pitiful dozen (mainly car ferries and small utility vessels) of the present. In 1900 there were forty-two paddle steamers and four screw vessels, capable of carrying over 50,000 passengers; in 1910 there were thirty-three paddle steamers and eight screw vessels, including the new turbines, with the same carrying capacity. Perhaps the peak year was 1906, when the daily passenger potential was 60,000 on every working day of the summer season. By contrast the present fleet can carry about a third of that number.

There were nearly seventy piers in operation, plus a dozen connecting ferry calls, against less than twenty today. Rothesay pier had over 100 daily steamer calls during the summer of 1913, compared with less than forty by 1960, and even fewer ten years later. And astonishingly the travel times more than matched those of subsequent years. In 1890 the combined rail and steamer journey from Glasgow to Rothesay was covered incredibly in 60min, a time that has never been bettered or even equalled. One of the strange features of Clyde steamship history is that progress has seemed at times to travel in the wrong direction. Although that amazing 1890 time could not be cited as a regular timetable pattern, it was accomplished on several occasions. Twenty years later, in 1910 the regular allotment for the journey was 80min, while in 1955 the standard schedule was 97min. The preponderance of car-ferry traffic makes a 1972 comparison difficult, but it can be said safely that speeds have not improved.

During the 1890s intense company and personal rivalry resulted in both train and boat races. This renewal of the earlier steamer races resulted in many exciting encounters. At that time there appeared to be at least tacit official approval for the contests, and the famous matches featuring the *Columba* and the *Lord of the Isles*, *Glen Sannox* and *Duchess of Hamilton*, *Galatea* and *Mercury*, and *Waverley* and *Jupiter*, have a place in steamer lore.

174

The epic struggles, especially those involving the *Columba* and the *Lord of the Isles* in their 10 o'clock daily dash for Rothesay pier, attracted crowds along the shore. In other races for the smaller piers of the Kyles of Bute and elsewhere speed was not the only factor, tactics playing an important part in manoeuvring and positioning for piers. It was difficult to tell whether those contests were enjoyed more by the passengers or the crews involved, but they certainly added an extra dimension to a sail on the Firth of Clyde.

Similar races persisted even into the 1930s, although they were then on a more modest scale, resulting from personal rivalry between individual ships and captains, and, unlike the earlier contests, were strictly without official approval.

Although not wholly within the province of the island, the county of Bute had a close interest in some unusual happenings on the neighbouring Isle of Cumbrae in 1906. That celebrated encounter between the steamship companies and the local Millport council arose over the vexed question of pier dues. The companies objected to what they considered exorbitant charges, which the council justified on the expenditure incurred for pier maintenance and improvement. At the start of the main holiday season steamer services were withdrawn, and intending holiday-makers left stranded. Scenes of almost carnival nature took place on Millport pier as the last steamer left to the accompaniment of sirens, cheers, and the playing of 'Will you no come back again?' by a brass band.

On a more practical level a motor launch service was arranged as Cumbrae settled down to life as a deserted island. For a time both sides remained adamant, but Lloyd George, as President of the Board of Trade, finally intervened, a compromise was found, and the siege ended conveniently just before the Glasgow holidays.

Pier dues provided a bone of contention for individuals as well as companies, and many an indignant Clydesider has made caustic comments on this surcharge. When excursion steamers disembarked their cruise passengers for a 15min stop at some remote Argyll pier, protesting voices were raised against the charge levied for the privilege of stepping out to examine the attractions of a wild landscape. What was said when the visitors, having exhausted the interest, returned a few minutes later to be met with demands for further payment for embarkation, may be left to the imagination. More than one Glasgow man has been known to comment that he had not intended to buy the so-and-so pier; but many another would now gladly pay his dues tenfold were those little piers still there to receive travellers.

Sunday boats, or Sabbath-breakers as they were known to diehard Observance champions, provided another controversial topic. The maintenance of strict Sunday Observance was no new problem for the island. In 1700 William Blair, the ferryman at Kilmichael, had been ordered under penalty not to row travellers over to Kames on the Sabbath unless 'they can evidence the same to be upon urgent necessitie', perhaps the first injunction or restriction against Sunday sailings.

For a long time the Firth of Clyde resorts held firm against the intrusions of Sunday excursionists. Attempts at sailings had been successfully resisted as far back as the 1850s, but it was 1897 before a serious challenge was made, and fiercely resisted. In that year the famous blockade of Dunoon was perhaps the most spectacular effort of passionate defiance, but most of the other coast towns expressed strong Sabbatarian views, with only the occasional concession of some liberal who expressed readiness to allow the sailings if a religious service was held on the boat. For a time feeling raged strongly, and as late as the 1920s, sermons against the Sunday boats were preached in Rothesay churches.

Occasionally, too, the idyll of those summer sailing days was disturbed by certain practical snags. Among the minor blemishes to cloud the blue skies of yesteryear was the problem of cinders and smoke. Modern examiners of old photographs of those

176

steamship days have been puzzled by the sight of a crowded afterdeck of a steamer sailing down the Clyde under a cloudless sky, with passengers firmly holding open umbrellas above their heads. The answer was neither idiosyncracy nor hallucinations about imaginary rainclouds, but the very real presence of showers of cinders and soot. Things came to a head in 1891 when the captains of both the *Columba* and the *Lord of the Isles* were convicted at Rothesay court of allowing excessive smoke and soot from the funnels of their ships. Such problems proved tantalisingly difficult to solve, and even in the 1930s it was no uncommon sight to see an afterdeck complement of passengers, who had gratefully settled in the sheltered stern a few minutes earlier, suddenly scuttle for safety as the cinders began to fall.

Over the years serious accidents have been surprisingly rare considering the amount of traffic on the Firth, and the occasional navigational difficulties of fog, awkward piers, and the sudden onslaught of squalls. Among the mishaps recorded were:

1890 Collision between *Scotia* and *Duchess of Hamilton*
1893 Rescue of man and child overboard at Rothesay Pier
1899 Steamer aground at Arran
1899 *Viceroy* sailing from Millport to Kilchattan Bay collided with Welsh steamship
1907 Loss of the *Kintyre* after collision with steamer doing trials on the measured mile off Skelmorlie. This was one of the rare serious accidents. The Rothesay steamers *Marchioness of Bute* and *Marchioness of Breadalbane* attended and lowered boats. The captain of the *Kintyre* was saved, but the chief engineer was drowned.
1935 *Duchess of Rothesay* sank
1936 *Duchess of Fife* aground

Such a representative list does not record the fairly frequent collisions with piers, the occasional encounters in fogs, minor alarms with rowing boats in Rothesay Bay, nor the more distant tragedies of well loved Clyde steamers who died 'in action' following Dunkirk, or on other wartime missions.

Perhaps the only Clyde spectacle to rival or supplement the

fleet of pleasure steamers was the great gatherings of yachts at the summer regattas. For many years the Clyde Fortnight in July was an important date in the yachting calendar. In 1891 over seventy yachts took part, and large crowds on the steamers followed the races. In 1893 the Prince of Wales was present with the royal yacht *Britannia*. One of the greatest assemblies, and most famous occasions, took place in glorious June weather during the Glasgow Exhibition of 1901, when again many of the Clyde steamers followed the yachts. Famous contestants included Thomas Lipton's *Shamrock*, and the German Kaiser's *Meteor*. When large-scale regattas were resumed between the wars, successors to the *Shamrock* were renowned contestants, and as late as the 1930s the last of the *Shamrocks* made one further attempt to win the America's Cup.

Royal visitors continued to patronise the yachting regattas. In 1920 George V followed his father's example by visiting Rothesay, while the link was continued after World War II when the Duke of Edinburgh participated.

STEAMER CRUISES

Although it would be an exaggeration to class the Clyde steamers as 'showboats', entertainment, and in particular music of various kinds, played a considerable part in some of the Clyde summer cruises. For many years the small group of entertaining musicians formed a recognisable and expected attraction on nearly every steamer—from the old German bands playing their Strauss waltzes to the more native groups of the 1920s and 1930s, complete with velvet collecting bag and repertoire of Hebridean tunes and Harry Lauder selections. A few steamer bands lingered on into postwar years, notably on the *Duchess of Hamilton* and *Queen Mary II*, but the best days had passed.

Before the turn of the century the idea of entertainment on board was being fully exploited. The *Clyde Programme* of 1898 featured the *Duchess of York* as the 'Musical Cruise Steamer', and advertised Henry Hayward's 'Musical Cruises and Al Fresco Concerts', publishing complete programmes for the entertainments that were to highlight those twice-daily cruises. Recurring musical favourites in the repertoire included *When Other Lips*, *Dreams on the Ocean*, and *Believe me if all these endearing young charms*.

In subsequent years various types of evening cruise were organised for the purpose of entertainment. In a fascinatingly nostalgic book, *Colour on the Clyde*, the late Cameron Somerville, who knew and loved his Clyde, has described the pattern of these sailings:

> What usually happened was this. A grand torchlight Evening Cruise starting from Rothesay was advertised simultaneously at Largs, Millport, Fairlie, and Kilchattan Bay, next Wednesday to Toward with pipe-band, dancing, torches etc., price of ticket 1/–. At 7–30 on that evening the *Kylemore* left with all her flags up and her band playing and went round the piers of the nearer Firth, at every one of which friends met friends with rapturous pleasure, the parties joined themselves to other groups, and the steamer became more and more crowded. At Toward the passengers would move in procession to a field nearby, and there to the piping of the band and in the smoky romantic light from the flaring torches dancing was held for an hour or so. The procession was then reformed, led by the band and illuminated by the wild light from the dying torches back to the ship.

In later years, with a similar pattern, the excursions became 'mystery cruises', with destinations like Keppel, Colintraive, or even an unnamed point. As Mr Somerville concludes:

> What could be more thrilling than to land on an Island at the Narrows, in the most beautiful part of the far-famed Kyles of Bute, when the brilliant splendour of the sunset is making one's heart ache at the wonderful scene of the dark shadows and glorious lights on the hills around, and the red reflections on the black waters at our feet, and to dance there with flambeaux and pipers while the darkness came slowly down. In the sunset the waters of the Kyles of Bute like a brilliant pathway into the glorious riot of colour to the west.

179

But surely the most spectacular Clyde cruise of all took place on a Sunday in June, during Glasgow's famous International Exhibition of 1901. The cruise was advertised as a 'grand al fresco concert by the Berlin Philharmonic Orchestra now appearing at the Exhibition, aboard the *Duchess of York* sailing to Rothesay and the far-famed Kyles of Bute'. In those times it appeared to be obligatory to refer to the Kyles of Bute as 'far-famed', but it must have been a rare experience to sail those delectable waters while listening to the strains of the Berlin Philharmonic.

After World War I entertainment was modest, but evening cruises to the various Illuminations and Fireworks Displays often included pipe band and Highland dancing performances, and occasionally entertainments by seaside concert parties. Even after World War II attempts to revive the 'showboat' idea were sponsored by newspapers with some success, but perhaps not sufficient to restore the glories and magic of a departed age.

It would be difficult to exaggerate the passion that many Clydesiders retain for those little ships that down the years have sailed the Firth. In many a conversation the names of the boats, old or new, are sounded liltingly on the tongue, and echoed in many conversations or daydreams; the *Caledonia*, the *Atalanta*, the *Columba*, and the *Lord of the Isles*—and if variation is required one can turn to the names of the long-lost piers, Ormidale and Kilchattan, Carradale, and Colintraive.

Alas, most of this belongs to the past, with nostalgia the only excuse for the recital! Apart from diminishing numbers, it is difficult to wax romantic over a car ferry or a terminal, however efficient the service they provide. George Blake, the author of several vivid and authentic Clydeside novels, including *The Shipbuilders*, examined the continuing legend in *The Firth of Clyde*, where he wrote of the reasons for the cult of those river steamers of the day before yesterday:

Many men not yet old were boys when the Firth of Clyde bubbled with action and colour, and they have seen during a brief space of historical time a vast number of levelling changes. They are in the same boat (the pun is accidental) with those who regret the passing of the Clippers on the high seas or the horse-drawn buses along the Strand. They are but nearly voiceless poets, almost inarticulately protesting against the ineluctable.

To cater for some of these poets, organisations like the Clyde River Steamer Club and the Paddle Steamer Preservation Society exist, and have large and enthusiastic memberships that are in no way diminished by the current decline in steamer traffic. From time to time one of the remaining few Clyde steamers is hired for a special cruise, while meetings, exhibitions, and other activities are organised to celebrate and perpetuate the inexhaustible theme.

There may be a danger that the steamer devotee in search of the lore and colour of the old loved boats thinks of them only as a special attraction for visitors, an inclusive part of the holiday scene, existing only as providers of pleasure, aesthetic or otherwise. Certainly that splendid Clyde Steamer fleet could not have existed in all its pride and complexity without the patronage of the holidaymaker, but there is another side to the picture.

THE ISLAND BOATS

A vital dimension would be lacking if the place of the Clyde steamer service in relation to the lives of the people of the Firth was not given consideration. For the islanders of Bute the steamers had a special role, completely separate from those periods of holiday traffic. And the connection with, and affection for, the little boats that carried them to and fro across the water in every season of the year was as strong as, and perhaps more intimate than, that of the amateur enthusiast from farther up the river.

To Rothesay folk the steamers were always there as an

integral part of their everyday life, carrying them on inter-island visits to friends or relatives, or on trips to the mainland for business or pleasure. They were used for 'flittings', when all the household gear travelled with its owners to the new home; they were used at weddings, when the ship was decorated with flags and bunting, and the skipper sounded a good-luck message from the siren; they were used at funerals, when the flags were lowered to half-mast in respect for a last voyage to the island. The children from Cumbrae and Arran came to their Rothesay school aboard those boats, the farmers used them to travel to marts or cattle shows with the beasts they had reared, and women on occasional shopping jaunts to the city shared the early morning sailing with daily commuters who could not be tempted to leave the island despite a job on the mainland.

First-footings and fair days, duty visits or family excursions, to and from Tarbert, Ardrishaig, Tighnabruaich, Innellan, Dunoon, Millport, Greenock, Largs, Wemyss Bay, and a dozen other places were always linked in the islander's mind with the essential boat-trip from Rothesay pier. The island traveller had a friendly but critical interest in the boats and their crew, more intimate, and perhaps more realistic than that of the summer holiday visitor, but none the less intense. For them the steamers were always there to carry them on their lawful occasions—all the year round, in fair or foul weather—and although they indulged the visitor's enthusiasm for the crowded summer piers, there was a deep sense that the steamers really belonged to Bute again when the last holiday excursion had sailed out of the bay.

THE LORE OF THE CLYDE

Something of the lore of the Firth of Clyde has been captured in literature, and in humorous vein few writers can match Neil Munro's collections of short stories and cameos concerning Para Handy, skipper of the aptly named puffer *The Vital Spark*.

Although Neil Munro won fame through his vivid novels of the Highlands—*Doom Castle, The New Road, John Splendid,* and *Gilian the Dreamer*—he was an admirer as well as the recorder of the places of the Clyde, and wrote of Bute as 'indented by beautiful sandy bays, traversed by lovely valleys with an expansive area of verdant foliage and sward. The mountains of Cowal fling fond arms round its head and comfort it against the northern winds; flowers flourish there that will grow nowhere else in Scotland, and strawberries and roses are sometimes seen blossoming in midwinter'.

Paradoxically it was not the reasoned appreciation of the Clyde that identified it indelibly with Neil Munro's name, rather was it through the appealing mixture of history, fantasy, colour, and humour which abounded in every episode of those chronicles of *The Vital Spark* and her intrepid skipper.

The creator of Para Handy was born at Inveraray in 1864 and died at Helensburgh in 1930. Between these points and within those years is contained much of the story of the Firth. Neil Munro noted every year from the 1860s, which saw the start of the popular Clyde Coast holiday, to the 1930s, when this tide was on the turn. Para Handy threw a rope across every pier from the Tail of the Bank to the head of Loch Fyne. *The Vital Spark* has lain fast in the mud at Colintraive, she has rounded Ardlamont in a sou'wester that set her decks awash. She has been reflected in the mirrored loch at Ormidale as she bumped softly against her fenders, she has rolled drunkenly in the Sound of Bute with a badly trimmed cargo of timber. To the mortification of her skipper she has taken a removal from Dunoon: 'fancy putting a flitting on the Fital Spark. You would think she was a coal-larry'. Para Handy even had notions of sharing the passenger trade with the *King Edward* and *Lord of the Isles*—until the episode of Wee Teeny. Seeing the child weeping sorely on Inveraray quay as the excursion steamer left, the gallant crew ferried the stranded lass back home to

Rothesay, only to discover that she had been staying at Inveraray with her grannie.

Every quay had a story, every port a ploy. At Campbeltown the Tar was wed, at Innellan Dougie's wife came aboard to stir up trouble. Crarae was the scene of the skipper's battle of wits with unwelcome lodgers, Brodick was the venue of the great Canary contest, and there were hilarious encounters at Tarbert fair. Visitors to the famous Kyles still turn their heads to see the gaily coloured rocks known as the Maids of Bute, but do they realise that Para Handy was the first man to paint them? (Incidentally they are now featured on the Ordnance map!) Natives of Furnace should know whether local dances are as lengthy as when the crew of *The Vital Spark* arrived 'in plenty of time for the baal at Furnace—it only started yesterday'. And is it still true that 'you don't need tickets for a Furnace baal if you ken the man at the door and talk the Gaelic at him'?

Some Loch Fyne men may have solved the herring mystery that perturbed Para Handy. 'The herrin' is a great mystery. The more you will be catchin' of them the more there is and when they're not in't it at aal, they're no there.' Nor did the engineer's attempt at scientific explanation satisfy the gallant skipper. 'Cycles! That's the worst of science it takes aal the credit away from the Creator. Cycles! When the herrin' was in Loch Fyne they stayed there all the time and only took a daunder now and then the length of Ballantrae.'

Skipper McFarlane was as proud of his little ship as a commodore of an ocean liner. Any suggestion that the puffer's speed was limited to 5 knots was sure to arouse an indignant denial. 'Six knots many a time between the Skate and Otter.' Hints of limitations to his own horizons could also put Para Handy on his mettle. 'I've had education', he would assert, 'and education gives you the nerve. If you have the nerve you can go round the world.' And to the engineer's snorted retort, 'You werena very far roon the world whatever o't', the skipper indignantly replied. 'Don't be making a display of your ignorance, McPhail. Not round the world Man. I was twice at Ulla-pool and wance at Londonderry. I'm not one of your dry-land sailors.'

A typical tale concerned the suspected disappearance over-board of one of the crew. Para Handy felt he must send a telegram breaking the news, but decided 'it will not do to break it too suddenly. Maybe we will send two telegrams. We'll say in the first—your son Colin left the boat today—and in the next—he is not coming back, he is drooned'. Then there was the epic of the dog Biler, the name itself an inspiration, deaf as a door but still able to take the measure of McPhail, and keep Para Handy off his own boat one night at Skipness.

The Para Handy stories still go into edition after edition as minor classics of the Clyde, not only for their fun, but because behind Neil Munro's humour is a deep feeling for the places of the Firth, and the golden days they knew.

On occasion real life has matched fiction, and a study of old newspaper files can produce a collection of anecdotes to add to the saga of the Clyde. Apart from races, and collisions in fog or with piers, there seemed always to be someone falling over-board—and happily always being rescued. Alan J. S. Paterson, in his colourful and evocative book *The Golden Years of the Clyde Steamers*, describes one such incident as reported in the *Glasgow Herald* of July 1893:

Just as the steamer *Mercury* was about to leave Rothesay pier, a middle-aged man, with a two-years old child, fell into the water. A young man named Joseph Maguire immediately leaped from the pier to the paddlebox and seized the man, who had been stunned by a blow on the head as he fell. On being assisted by some others to pull the man out, he immediately dived after the child, who by this time had disappeared under the water. In a few seconds he came to the surface, bringing with him the child alive, and little the worse for its immersion, amid the ring-ing cheers of thousands on the pier and steamer. A substantial subscription was collected from the passengers by a gentleman on board, and presented to the rescuer by the captain.

THE ISLAND OF BUTE

The classic sequence of accident, rescue, cheers from the crowd, whip-round, and presentation by the captain, was repeated many a time in fact and fantasy. Occasionally there were variations, real or apocryphal. Perhaps the most told tale is of the rescuer at Rothesay pier, who, after a brave and hazardous rescue, delivered the youngster who had been saved from a watery grave to his mother, and was greeted with the stern query, 'Where's his bunnet?' At one time the number of children falling off Rothesay pier or harbour must have neared epidemic proportions, and young rescuers frequently remained anonymous, their only recognition being a parental rebuke for coming home with their clothes drenched.

FAMOUS STEAMERS

Many of the individual Clyde steamers have fascinating life stories, and some retain a permanent place in the history of navigational development. The story of the *Columba* is in itself a minor saga. One of the most famous, and easily the largest steamer ever to sail on the Clyde passenger service, the *Columba* was launched at Clydebank in 1878, and sailed regularly for fifty-eight seasons before being broken up in 1936. She was 300ft long and 27ft broad, only the second Clyde steamer to be built of steel, and she carried 2,190 passengers and crew. Officially registered at Lloyd's as a smack, she used her sails regularly in the early years, particularly on the Loch Fyne passage. (It is worthy of note that many Clyde steamers including the *Galatea*, carried sails until as late as 1907.) *Columba*'s huge and impressive round paddle-boxes, with the name boldly painted and adorned by a thistle growing out of the letter U, became famous sights on the Firth, and she was a familiar daily visitor to Rothesay pier throughout her career.

The *Columba* had a top speed of 19 knots—and needed it to cover her remarkable daily schedule. For over 30 years before World War I she left Glasgow Broomielaw at 7 am, calling at

Partick, Govan, the two Greenock piers, Gourock, Kirn, Dunoon, and Innellan, before often racing the *Lord of the Isles* for the 10.15 Rothesay berth. After Bute there were further calls at Colintraive, Tighnabruaich, Auchenlochan, Ardlamont, and Tarbert, before arrival at the Ardrishaig terminus.

Some of *Columba*'s distinctive features helped to add to the legend. Her barber's shop was unique to a Clyde steamer, and surprisingly remained in existence until 1931; it was well equipped with rotary hairbrush and other refinements, and could even offer a bath to weary travellers. At one time, when there was no hairdresser in Ardrishaig, local residents sailed to Tarbert for the purpose of having their hair cut on the *Columba*. After the service was withdrawn, a Greenock barber sailed with the ship at regular intervals, cutting the hair of the crew during the voyage. The bookstall and fruitstall were less exclusive features, being common to several Clyde steamers, but the *Columba*'s Post Office, which existed until 1915, was a distinctive service, although not a pioneering one, as the *Lord of the Isles* had forestalled her rival in this field.

It should be remembered also that in addition to her popular passenger service the *Columba* was the mail steamer and an important carrier of goods, functioning as a vital connecting link for the Kyles of Bute, east and west Kintyre, Crinan, and the inner and outer islands of the west. Over her long service she had only four masters and two pursers, all well known figures on the Clyde.

Perhaps the *King Edward* was next to the *Columba* in popularity and importance. Launched in 1901, she was the first commercial turbine steamer in the world, and her trials aroused great interest among marine designers, engineers, and shipping chiefs. Her speed of over 20 knots fully justified the confidence of the inventor and sponsor, and her continued success on the Camp-beltown run paved the way for further development in steam propulsion, and impressive advances in marine design. The *King Edward* sailed for 50 years, and after she was broken up in

187

1952, her famous three turbine engines were preserved and displayed in the shipping section of Kelvingrove Museum.

Cameron Somerville, who knew so many of the ships, enthused particularly about the *Glen Sannox*, 'the loveliest of all the Clyde steamers. Her long graceful lines, her tall pencil funnels speaking of speed and elegance, the flowing curves of her white and gold paddle-boxes, her most attractive colour scheme— red, white, and blue-grey—all made a picture of beauty that long lingered in the mind'. Many who knew the *Glen Sannox* would agree, while others may judge from the handsome colour plate that forms the frontispiece to Alan Paterson's *The Golden Years of the Clyde Steamers.*

Among the many worth more than a passing mention are the *Galatea*, the old flagship of the Caledonian fleet with two distinctive and widely separated funnels, whose memory is preserved by a Rothesay pub of that name, and many a small-scale model; the *Ivanhoe*, known far and wide as the 'teetotal boat', and less likely to have a pub named after her on that account; the little *Lucy Ashton*, whose career spanned 60 years; the two-funnelled *Queen Alexandra*, who became the three-funnelled *Saint Columba* after renovation; the *Queen Mary*, built in 1932, who gracefully changed her name to *Queen Mary II*, when her larger if not older sister, the first of the famous Cunard Queens, was launched a few years later—incidentally the Clyde steamer has outlived her greater namesake by continuing to sail as one of the last of the old Clyde favourites.

The skippers often had as much character as the ships they commanded. Standing on the bridge wearing gold braid, with whiskers bristling, they were masters of their craft in every sense. Stories of their encounters with rival captains, pier officials, passengers, and even the law, are numerous. Captain Robert Morrison of the old *Duchess of Hamilton* and Captain Colin McGregor of the *Glen Sannox* were prominent at the time of the races of the 1890s, and more than once found themselves in trouble through the competitive urge. Captain Angus

Campbell was a renowned skipper of the *Columba*, while Captain McKellar of the *Galatea* also made an impressive appearance. In *Glimpses of Rothesay* the author portrayed one of these nine-teenth-century worthies, Captain William Buchanan, recording that like many another he had a 'wee failing' in his love of the bottle. However, the author asserts that 'drunk or sober he could read his titles clear to mansions in the skies'—but does not say anything about his navigation in these circumstances.

What is left for the Clyde steamer enthusiast who wants more than nostalgia, and prefers even the limited excursions of the present to the legendary voyages of the past? The superb and unique scenery of the Firth of Clyde has been affected sur-prisingly little by modern development, and given time and a little ingenuity most of the routes can still be covered by steamer. Loch Long, Loch Goil, Arran and Cumbrae, Campbeltown and Inveraray, trips through the Kyles and round Bute, all feature in the current summer programme, and although many of the little piers are derelict and rotting, the bays and lochs are still open to the last of the old ships.

Although the *Waverley* is not so old as one or two of the others, she remains, since the much lamented departure of the *Caledonia*, the world's last seagoing paddle steamer, and because she is something of a symbol of the past great efforts are being made to keep her in service as long as possible. Company officials, recognising perhaps belatedly that there are commercial possibilities in exploiting uniqueness, strive to maintain the vessel in service, despite the problems of running costs, naviga-tional deficiencies, and maintenance difficulties. Of course, the diehard enthusiasts of the Steamer clubs, together with many other devotees of the Clyde, hope that her paddles will continue to churn for a while at least.

No longer is there a service from Broomielaw to cater for Glasgow's all-the-way enthusiasts, and the joys of sailing past the shipyards to the sound of the riveters have disappeared. Rothesay's day-long procession of steamers, making the bay alive with boats, is only a memory. The *Caledonia* and the *Duchess of Hamilton* have gone, and there is only one survivor of the prewar fleet to awaken memories of halcyon days, and recapture the atmosphere of former busy times.

At the end of an era the temptation is to sigh for its passing, but full mourning for the little ships of the Clyde would at least be premature, for although the present sailing pattern bears little resemblance to the golden days, at least there are still steamers on the Firth.

11   THE OTHER SIDE OF BUTE

I N much of the story of Bute, Rothesay has been the focal
point, but there are places on the periphery that have played
their part in the island's development. Through varied
contributions, and with widely differing roles, Port Bannatyne,
Kilchattan, Mount Stuart, Straad, and Inchmarnock merit
our attention.

PORT BANNATYNE

Port Bannatyne, a village that at the height of its development
had a population close on 2,000, is Bute's largest centre of
population outside Rothesay. Although it has shared in many
of the larger town's enterprises and services, the Port has also
retained its own individuality. It was an important link in the
island's tramway system, first as the terminus for the early
horse-cars, and later as a connecting junction for the electric
cars on the Ettrick Bay route.

During the earlier days of Bute's cotton boom, spinning
wheels were in use in many Port Bannatyne houses, but the
introduction of the power loom soon destroyed this practice.

The ideal anchorage provided by a deep-set bay was
extensively used to supplement Rothesay's harbour, and over
the years it has been a popular mooring for yachts and other
small craft. Much larger ships have taken advantage of the
natural shelter, particularly in the trade recession of the 1930s,
and during World War II, while even to the present day the
occasional large tanker can be seen at anchor over a period.

Port Bannatyne steamer pier was a busy centre during the prosperous years of Firth of Clyde sailings. It was the terminus for the popular yellow-funnelled Caledonian fleet, had been the headquarters of Captain Williamson's well known trio of steamers, the *Sultan, Sultana,* and *Viceroy,* and remained a regular port of call for the Kyles of Bute and Loch Fyne excursions. The steamer pier was closed before World War II, and is now derelict, while the nearby stone pier is little used, but the continued presence of many yachts and small boats maintains the bay's colourful scene, and the local boatyards seem as busy as ever.

The district's long history can be traced back to the founders of the Bannatyne family of Kames. The earliest record refers to the vesting of the estate in the name of John, son of Gilbert, around 1334, and there is some evidence that this may have been the same John who was in command of Rothesay Castle under Edward Baliol. Kames Castle, the seat of the Bannatynes, was built in the fourteenth century, and is one of the oldest continuously inhabited houses in Scotland; but it has been extensively altered, only the square tower indicating something of the original. The tall turreted keep of Wester Kames is also a good example of old Scottish architecture, though that also was reconstructed, for occupation by the fourth marquess in 1905.

The main development of Port Bannatyne in its present form took place between 1890 and 1910, when there was something of a building boom, and many houses, including rows of tenements, were constructed. At that time efforts were made to project the village as an independent holiday resort, with attractions that included a magnificent hydropathic, a picturesque sea front, and a good steamer service. It was just before this period that the Marquess of Bute, having acquired the lands of Kames, changed the name of the village from Kamesburgh to Port Bannatyne, the aim being to perpetuate the name of the original family.

Kilchattan Bay at the time of the *New Statistical Account* was a quiet fishing village with about fifty small cottages. Until the second half of the nineteenth century Kilchattan was thought of as a remote, rather picturesque backwater, where most of the villagers had their own cow with some grazing on the hill and along the shore. Several local fishermen used the sheltered harbour as anchorage for their boats; and a meal mill on the same site as an old fifteenth-century mill was in use until the 1880s. In 1840 there were three schools and six alehouses in the parish, serving a population of just over 800. In 1849 a tileworks was built, and this industry persisted until 1915, employing an average of twenty men. Although there was no other main occupation outside those mentioned, tourism began in the mid-nineteenth century. The village's attractive setting in a wide sandy bay encouraged early holidaymakers, and, with the erection of the pier and hotel in the last quarter of the nineteenth century, Kilchattan became a sizeable holiday resort, with its own steamer service from Wemyss Bay, Fairlie, and Millport, and daily calls from excursion steamers. Villas and tenements were built, an anchorage for small boats provided, and the Bay became a most popular summer resort, its long spell of seasonal prosperity reaching a peak in the 30 years before World War I but surviving in a modified form in modern times. With the decline of the local fishing industry and the closing of the tileworks, tourism and agriculture provided the only occupations.

Outside Kilchattan Bay the parish of Kingarth is composed of agricultural land, some woodland, and stretches of hill and moorland. Perhaps the richest and most beautiful part of Bute, the south end is also strong in archaeological and historical relics, with the church of St Blane's and the vitrified fort at Dunagoil outstanding. There are several interesting geological features in the neighbourhood, including the beds of upper old red sandstone, which account for Kilchattan's sandy bay and the light soil so beneficial to the growing of early potatoes. The volcanic crags of the south are impressive, and the presence and form of the patch of columnar sandstone near Kilchattan Bay pier has posed an interesting problem for experts. At the south end of the village, at Hawk's Neb point, the remains of Ganoid fishes, estimated to be 200 million years old, have been found.

In contrast to other parts of the island where 'incomers' now exceed 'natives' in number, the majority of the inhabitants of Kingarth parish are of local origin and descent. In early times this was the most populous part of the island, and right up to the Middle Ages the lands of Kingarth had a distinct independence of their own. In the oldest records the heritors of the parish are referred to as 'Barons', a term used throughout Bute but not in this sense outside the island. They were descendants of the tenants who had been granted a charter by James IV in 1506, and interestingly the farm names mentioned in these documents have been retained to the present day.

One of these families, the McCaws of Garrochty, had been prominent in south-west Bute since the reign of Alexander III and were among the names mentioned in the 1506 charter. While other lands were being 'disponed' to the Stewart family, the McCaws retained their full independence right on to 1845, and even to the present day Garrochty is a notable exception to the general rule of Bute Estate control.

Education, too, has a long history in the Kingarth parish. As early as 1649 the Kirk Session took steps to found a school, which came into being the following year. A succession of interesting if not always distinguished schoolteachers followed; they were mostly masters, but one woman who was appointed had the misfortune to be called before the session on more than one occasion for 'flyting and drinking'. The Session kept close control of school and teachers as long as their power remained.

It kept watch on social occasions, too, and an extract of December 1658 ordained 'for the better regulating of disorders that fall out at Penny Brydelles appoint that there be no piping, no promiscuous dancing under the penaltie of the parties maryed losing their consignation money and that there be no sitting up to drink after 10 o'clock at night under the fine of forty shillings to be paed by the master of the family where the Brydell holds'.

Road transport from Kilchattan to Rothesay appears to have been slow in adapting to modern conditions. During the first two decades of the twentieth century the horse-bus service had alternative vehicles for winter and summer. The winter coach, irreverently described as the 'Tinker's Tent', resembled a prairie waggon in its canvas covering. The floor was straw-covered, interior lighting consisted of a candle, and the vehicle carried livestock as well as passengers. The summer alternative, an elaborate four-in-hand manned by 'red-coated guard complete with bugle', was more comfortable as well as more elegant, but the journey took a leisurely $1\frac{1}{2}$hr to complete. These famous Kilchattan coaches were not replaced by motor vehicles until 1919.

MOUNT STUART

For nearly six centuries the Stewart family have played a major part in the development of Bute, and during the last two and a half centuries the successive earls and marquesses have maintained residence in the Mount Stuart estate.

One of the earlier records in 1400 announces King Robert III's confirmation of his father's grant of lands and the hereditary office of Sheriff of Bute to John Stewart. Almost a century later, in 1498, King James IV added the office of hereditary Captain and Keeper of Rothesay Castle. When the castle was finally destroyed in 1685, the Bute family lived for a time in the old Mansion House in the High Street opposite. This house, which was built in 1680, has been finely restored to serve as Bute Estate Office.

The second Earl of Bute had many ideas and plans for building the great house at Mount Stuart, and also developing the grounds, for even before the foundations were laid young trees and seeds were being gathered. The accounts for those items supplied by William Miller, the Holyrood Abbey seedsman in 1717, included items like 'starhus arabia, double sunflour, pompion, sweet basile, dill, melon, amoranthus, marvell of peru, hysop, tobacco seed, double holeyoak, African marigold; pear, apple, cherrie plumb and roun trees, 4000 thorns, 10 whyt and 10 red Dutch currans, severall kindes of Roses, 500 Beeches, 1000 green Holleys, and 100 plants liquorish, 16 Pyramid Yew trees, 1000 young yews', while later accounts include many more trees, paradise stocks, asparagus, and fig trees.

Here was the foundation of the famous garden and trees of Mount Stuart. After several delays the building of the house was finally begun in 1718, and the work was virtually completed four years later, although its originator lived only a few months to enjoy the fruition of his long-considered plans; but his successor, the third Earl of Bute, inherited his father's feeling for the island, and especially the house and grounds at Mount Stuart.

The third Earl was probably the most influential of all the Butes. As tutor to George III he was in a powerful position, and as a favourite of the young king eventually achieved notable success as a Tory minister. Reputedly against his own wishes he accepted the post of prime minister, and by the irony of fate made himself one of the most unpopular prime ministers who ever held office.

After 1744 political activities forced him to administer Bute Estate through commissioners and agents. He made a number of additions to the house, and provided substantial annual outlays for the gardens. Throughout his life, his interest in Mount Stuart remained keen—the foremost architects, including one of the renowned Adams, were employed on house improvements, and the best gardening experts were consulted about the grounds.

Among the eighteenth-century visitors was Mr Pennant, who published a book of his 'Tour', and described Mount Stuart as 'a modern house with a handsome front and wings; the situation very fine, on an eminence in the midst of a wood, where trees grow with as much vigor as in the more Southern parts—and Throstles, and other birds of song, fill the groves with their melody'.

This interest in Mount Stuart was maintained by the fourth Earl, who became the first Marquess, and by the second Marquess, who, with his wife, designed new gardens and developed the attractive village of Kerrycroy.

An interesting link between past and present is found in the *Lady Guildford*, a barge built in 1819 to carry the marquess's bride from the mainland to Mount Stuart, the crew 'appropriately' wearing specially designed tartan. The *Lady Guildford*, a beautiful little vessel, remained afloat until 1939, and can still be seen in McIntyre's Boatyard at Port Bannatyne, looking as if she could take to the water again without any worry.

By 1840 the Bute family had achieved something of an autocracy in Bute, owning six-sevenths of the land and exerting influence in many spheres. The second Marquess had also consolidated the family's wealth through his successful investments in founding the port of Cardiff and developing property there. Unexpectedly his successor took a completely different course.

John Patrick, the third Marquess of Bute (1847–1900) was undoubtedly one of the most sensitive and intelligent of the Bute family, a man of great culture and widespread interests, but ironically his own integrity of character led him to actions that aroused tremendous criticism and opposition locally and nationally. As a young man at Oxford he became deeply concerned with religious questions and formed a close friendship with Monsignor Capel, a devout follower of Cardinal Newman's movement. After much heartsearching the young Marquess became convinced at the age of twenty that he must renounce the Protestant faith and become a Roman Catholic. Extracts from some of the letters he wrote at the time are revealing and obviously sincere:

> I came to see very clearly indeed that the Reformation was in England and Scotland the work neither of God nor of the people, its real authors being in the former country a lustful and tyrannical King and in the latter a pack of greedy, time-serving and unpatriotic nobles . . . I also convinced myself (1) that while the disorders rampant in the Church during the sixteenth century clamoured loudly for reform, they in no way justified apostacy and schism; and (2) that were I personally to continue under this or any other pretext to remain outside the Catholic and Roman church I should be making myself an accomplice after the fact in a great national crime and the most indefensible act in history. And I refuse to accept any such responsibility.

The decision was a great blow to the family and connections, who strongly suspected Jesuit influence, and they did everything in their power to prevent the change of faith. The young Marquess wanted to enter the Catholic Church at Easter 1867, but tremendous pressure was put on him to postpone the final step at least until after his twenty-first birthday. This partial success was referred to in a letter from the Marquess to Miss Skene, dated Maundy Thursday 1867: 'The Protestants i.e. the Lord Chancellor and his Court; my Guardian; my friends and relations; and Mensel Lidden and Co. have extorted from me a promise not to become a Catholic till I am of age. They are jubilant with the jubilation of devils over a lost soul; but I am hopeless and weary to a degree'.

To soften his bitter disappointment at the delay the young Marquess went on a pilgrimage in quest of the relics of St Magnus, visiting the little Orkney island of Egilsay where Magnus was slain by Haco in 1116. He landed there, kissed the sacred ground, and visited the ancient church, before going to the famous cathedral at Kirkwall. During the rest of his life Lord Bute 'Cherished a lively devotion and veneration for St. Magnus'.

The coming-of-age celebrations were held with full pomp and ceremony at Cardiff, but the Marquess held firm in his intentions, and the conversion took place in 1868. The year's delay appears to have done little to allay the strong reactions. Antagonism in Bute towards the young peer's change of religion was even stronger and more resentful than elsewhere. The *Buteman* devoted a full page to strong criticism of the landowner's action. Mainland newspapers were also outspoken and censorious. The *Daily News* reported that he 'had taken up his honours, wealth and influence and laid them in the lap of the Church of Rome', adding 'of course it is always a pity when a man believes too much in religion'. The *Glasgow Herald* suspected persuasion and affirmed, 'it is most likely this perversion is a result of priestly influences'. *The Scotsman* was rather more tolerant, believing that 'even those who most deeply regret the decision must admit it was made at great sacrifice and under the influence only of conscience'.

The third Marquess retained this strong faith throughout his life, making several pilgrimages to the Holy Land. On his return to Mount Stuart he made great efforts to win the affection and approval of the islanders. He took an active part in the preservation and restoration of the island's relics of the past, an example that has been followed by his successors. He was instrumental in preserving the ancient chapel of St Blane's, rebuilding part of it in 1896, when a portion of the causeway was excavated and foundations of early buildings were found.

He had wide interests and enthusiasms for subjects as diverse as philology and home rule for Scotland. He wrote poetry, was a keen historian and a prominent contributor to the *Scottish Review*. After the disastrous fire of 1877 he supervised the rebuilding of Mount Stuart House. He bought Falkland Palace in 1887 and Pluscarden Priory in 1897 with a view to preserving and restoring them, and the work at the Priory has been continued successfully over the years.

The Marquess also served as provost of Rothesay and rector of St Andrew's University. A study of his life and work reveals him as 'a man steeped in history, possessed of great imagination and learning, and most profoundly religious'.

The third Marquess died in October 1900, and, in accordance with his wish to be buried in the chapel in the grounds of Mount Stuart, his body was transported across the Firth of Clyde to Kilchattan Bay. A large crowd of mourners followed the coffin 5 miles on foot to the Mount Stuart chapel. 'Through russet and gold of the October woods it passed, night was falling as the cortege reached the little chapel on the shore and the pine torches threw sombre glare.' Vespers were sung and black-robed sisters watched the bier all night until requiem mass next morning. A few days later Lord Bute's widow, daughter and three sons set off to the Holy Land to inter the heart in the soil of Olivet.

The rebuilding of Mount Stuart continued for many years before the new house, incorporating the original north and south wings, was complete, although some details of the originator's plan were never finished. A noteworthy feature of the new building is the Chapel, with a tower designed as a replica of that of Saragossa Cathedral. Among the treasures of the library are thirteenth-century Greek Gospels, illuminated manuscripts, a unique Scottish collection complete with Kilmarnock Burns, collections of Royal letters, and sets of the third Earl's botanical studies. The picture galleries contain portraits by Reynolds, Raeburn, and Allan Ramsay, and paintings by Rubens and Kneller. Fine examples of stained glass, and Adam fireplaces and furniture are other items of interest.

The fourth Marquess continued the restoration work, and the present Marquess, in addition to his business interests on the island, maintains Mount Stuart and its treasures. As chairman of the National Trust for Scotland, the Marquess is a keen supporter of preservation and conservation. His continued interest in Rothesay Castle helped towards the reopening of the Great Hall in 1970, and other improvements have been made to the ancient castle, which is now in the care of the Secretary of State for Scotland.

The little village of Straad on the west coast of Bute, is hardly noticeable now as a centre of population; yet up to the end of the nineteenth century it was a self-contained community, and, together with the neighbouring Ballianlay lands, formed a distinctive part of the island.

Apart from the busy harbour and thriving group of herring and white-fishing boats, the Straad once had its joiner, cooper, blacksmith, two cobblers, and miller, and there were two licensed inns in the neighbourhood. At one time several large sailing smacks were based in St Ninian's Bay, where the wide sweep of water makes an attractive seascape, with Inchmarnock just over a mile beyond the point and Arran 9 miles away to the south-west. This shore has been blessed with many names over the years—the Straad, St Ninian's, the Cockle Shore, the Skerrel Shore. The kippering of herrings was first carried on at St Ninian's Point, and it is on record that several Straad men served with the tea clippers, including the *Thermopylae*.

At one time donkeys were kept by nearly everyone in St Ninian's Bay and the Straad, being used mainly for transporting fish to Rothesay. The animals used to be sent across for rest and summer grazing to Inchmarnock, and on one occasion it was noted that four of them swam back across the Firth.

The area has some interesting historical associations, and the excavations on St Ninian's Point attracted interest locally. To mark the 1,500th anniversary of the dedication of St Ninian's Chapel, a service was held on the site. In the same year as the Battle of Largs it is on record that a raiding party of Norsemen attacked Kilmory Castle, whose remains can be seen beside the farm of the same name; this was the Crowner's Castle, whose owners had summary power of arrest, charge, and sentence over those in their demesne.

The oldest inhabited house in the district is Stewart Hall, which was built in 1760 and is a fine example of mid-Georgian architecture. It was built for James Stewart, a descendant of the first Stewarts of Bute, who was one of the jurors in the notorious trial of James of the Glen for the murder of George Campbell, the Red Fox. Of the more recent occupiers of Stewart Hall, Dr Marshall, a prominent surgeon and co-founder of Bute Natural History Society, is well remembered.

The local school, Ballianlay, was one of the first to be built and served the community well until its final closure in 1966. The ruins of the old Greenan mill can still be seen. There was an inn there until 100 years ago, but it was not so well known as the Straad's 'Cockle Tavern'. The newest house in the vicinity was built in 1896, so no new buildings have been completed this century.

The last common grazing in Bute was at St Ninian's Bay, but this ancient right was recently forfeited on renting to a local farm. Until this century the pattern was for the cottars to have a small plot and common grazing for a cow and follower.

The inhabitants had a fair measure of prosperity and independence right up to the end of the last century, but with the passing of the old trades and activities, and the final closing of the school, only a little post office remains as a sign of an independent community.

INCHMARNOCK

Inchmarnock, the delectable isle of the old saints, shares with the southern parts of Bute the advantages of mild climate, sheltered shore, and light fertile soil, but it also has a unique appeal of its own. This may come partly from the heritage of the past in legend or history, and partly from the indefinable attractions of smallness and remoteness.

The island is 2½ miles in length, ½ mile in breadth, with an area of approximately 675 acres—and is as cut off as the remotest outposts of the Hebrides. There is no telephone or mail service, no pier or jetty, and, apart from two small outboard-engined boats used by the farmers of North Park and Mid Park, no contact with the outside world. Such a situation may seem surprising in an island less than 40 miles from the city of Glasgow, and separated from Bute by just over a mile of water. But this narrow strip of the Firth has treacherous currents and is subject to sudden squalls. In the winter of 1971–2, admittedly an unusually difficult period for high winds, the tenant of Mid Park was able to cross to Bute only once during the month of November, twice during December, and once in February. Isolation of this kind, involving the problems of ferrying all supplies by small boat, is not usually associated with life in the Firth of Clyde, and Inchmarnock's survival as an inhabited island remains something of an achievement.

For its size Inchmarnock has a surprising variety of wild life. It is exceptionally rich in wildflowers, including scarlet pimpernel, campion, thrift, the rare oyster flower, and a profusion of giant primroses. There are no large trees, but birch, hazel, and rowan grow well. Seals can be seen in the waters around it, particularly near the little tidal island of Tra-na-luie, and basking sharks up to 30ft long or more are not uncommon. The seas are rich in haddock, cod, and plaice, providing excellent line fishing.

Above all Inchmarnock remains an island of birds. Gulls, skuas, terns, curlews, pigeons, buzzards, peregrines, shags, and a variety of ducks, including goosanders, mallards, teal, and many others, add to the profusion of wings in the skies over the island, a feature that has been noted by visiting travellers throughout the ages. J. A. Gibson's notes on the breeding of birds on Inchmarnock, reported in the Buteshire Natural History Society's *Transactions* of 1969, makes interesting comparisons with earlier surveys on the island in 1938 and 1952. He indicates the presence of dabchicks, fulmar, shags, teal, buzzards, peregrines, and corncrakes, and reports a striking increase in eider duck, a steady increase in greater blackbacked gulls, and a spectacular increase in the lesser blackbacked variety.

Inchmarnock's herring gullery, which is easily the largest in the Clyde, continues to increase, but a slight decrease was noted in terns, wheatear, stonechat and peregrine falcons.

Inchmarnock's history has many fascinating aspects, and part of the strong appeal lies in the fact that the story is still being built up almost from day to day. The proportion of this small island's exhibits in the Bute Natural History Museum is impressive. Pride of place goes to the famous Inchmarnock necklace, already mentioned (see p 45). Also on exhibition in the museum is the shaft of a cross taken from the wall adjoining the burying ground of the chapel of St Marnoc. On one side are carved three crosses in saltire, and on the other either the shaft of a cross or the blade of a sword. There is also a fragment of sculptured stone from the chapel. Further discoveries were made by the young sons of the tenant of Mid Park, who in the spring of 1972 found two stones with ancient crosses, which await expert examination but appear similar to those previously found and dated approximately between 500 and 900 AD.

St Marnoc came to the 'delicious island' of Inchmarnock probably in the early seventh century, and the remains of the first monastic settlement and old burials can still be seen. It has been suggested that an early monastery on the island may have been attached to the Cistercian monastery of Saddell in Kintyre, and there may have been a connection with the settlement at St Ninian's, the nearest point on the Bute mainland. The island is called Mernock in Timothy Pont's 1622 Map of Bute. At one time there must have been fairly extensive slate quarries, and it has been said that Inchmarnock was for a period a notorious haunt of smugglers. In the early nineteenth century the population was twenty-two, and this number remained fairly constant for over 100 years, during which time the same families occupied the farms. One of the farmers, Charles McFie, who was a renowned wit, is reported, when having difficulty in hiring local labour, to have gone to Glasgow for feeing purposes, telling the applicants that the place of work was 'just a step' from the Straad. Tales are told of the consternation when Glasgow workers realised they had to cross 1½ miles of rough water in a small boat, with the prospect of not getting off the island for six months.

In addition to the summer visits of the Straad donkeys, it is on record that some strong drinkers from Bute were sent to Inchmarnock for a cure—or a punishment—and for a time it was known as the drunkard's isle.

In 1943 the government evacuated the people of Inchmarnock, and used it as a target for long-range gunfire, using live ammunition. This might have been the end of the story, for the odds against the survival of anything of the old way of life after those war years were great, but now its two remaining farms, North Park and Mid Park (South Park was rather mysteriously burned down after the army had given up control, but before agricultural working had been resumed), are tenanted and worked again. Despite the problems, modern mechanised farming is in operation, and the farmhouses have electric plants and up-to-date solid-fuel cookers. The present tenants under the Bute Estate are Mr Daniel Boag at North Park, and Mr Roderick Middleton at Mid Park. The Middleton family, who came to the island in 1967, partly to fulfil a longstanding ambition of Mr Middleton's, have restored an atmosphere of excitement, activity and adventure. The six children and their parents seem so naturally in tune with the small-island way of life that all the chores of working on the land or with boats, collecting fuel, tending the livestock, and collecting the various harvests of the seasons, seem part of a pattern that scarcely distinguishes between work and play, between learning and doing. Mr Boag discovered the Bronze Age cists on his land, and helped towards the important excavations which produced the Inchmarnock necklace and other relics.

The Inchmarnock farmers accept the restrictions imposed on them, knowing the hazards of taking eighty sheep in relays across the water by small boat, or even swimming pigs over to the nearest mainland point, but they may still hope for an improved landing-place on the island. If the transport problems could be solved, there might be potential in growing potatoes for early marketing, for the soil is as suitable as in the highly favoured south end of Bute, and in postwar years there was an Inchmarnock experiment in growing virus-free potatoes on virgin land.

In the meantime the two farmers of Inchmarnock are content to continue the story of Marnoc's isle, and keep its age-old record of human habitation intact at least for a little longer.

THE ISLAND'S CHARACTER
& PROBLEMS

IN some ways Bute appears to have been bypassed by the more spectacular changes of the century, and perhaps because of this it remains in the mind as the symbol of an island oasis in the modern expanse of developing Clydeside. Certainly it is remarkable that a small island within 30 miles of Glasgow, centre of one of the heaviest industrial concentrations in the world, threatened by the proximity of nuclear reactors, oil terminals, giant harbour complexes, and Polaris bases, and a natural target for tourist invasions, should retain so much of the peace usually associated with far more remote places.

Part of the secret may lie in the feeling of long years of history and prehistory which lingers around the island, beside the graves of those first Neolithic men, by the shores visited by early missionaries, amid the ruins of the abbeys of the saints or castle of the kings—for it is doubtful if there is a single spot on Bute which is not within sight of a place of archaeological or historical interest. Part may lie in the sense of continuity, which joins past to present, through the nearer legacy of ancestors who farmed the fertile lands, and fished the surrounding seas; and part may come from the policy of preservation and conservation followed with successful determination by the chief landowner, a policy that has been criticised and opposed by some, but one that may have prevented a few of the worst excesses of 'progress'.

Although the significance of the island's proximity to Glasgow should not be underestimated, there is the countering factor that although Bute's economy is closely linked to the

Central Lowlands, many of its characteristics remain Highland. Indeed Gaelic was spoken in north Bute until the end of the nineteenth century, and the island retains traditionally and historically an association with the Highlands and Islands.

Whatever the reasons for the near-miraculous survival of an area of peace in such an easily accessible region, the abundantly rich sea-bird sanctuaries, the quiet unspoiled sandy beaches, and the expanse of lonely deserted moorland, epitomise the atmosphere of Bute for many who know and love the island. Yet they realise that these qualities are precarious in a world which increasingly demonstrates the vulnerability of all quiet places in face of increasing urbanisation, and feel that the passing of all sense of remoteness may come for Bute, as it has for many former retreats, if not at the drop of a hat, perhaps with the building of a bridge.

It may be, too, that a very strong case can be made for such an event as one desirable for the general well-being of the island, for no community can exist entirely on a legacy from the past. But the double paradox remains that the very quality which attracts the visitor may be lost in too vigorous an attempt to make his journey easier. The choice is no simple one, for the presence of these visitors in sufficient numbers is a fundamental requirement for the prosperity of the island. Possibly there is a middle way, but at the moment the balance remains a delicate and chancy one.

Facts have to be faced even by 'delectable islands', and there would be no point in ignoring warning signals, or turning a blind eye to obvious trends. In 1971 Malcolm MacDonald produced a thorough and well documented thesis for Strathclyde University, entitled *The Island of Bute*, and sub-titled *A Study in Decline*. Apart from an inclination to see the problem and a suggested remedy *solely* from an economic point of view, and a tendency to equate decline with decay, Mr MacDonald's observations are shrewd, and his points well taken. He points out that 'the island's problems are the result of inability to make similar progress to that being made by mainland communities'. The generalisation prompts the question, 'Which mainland communities?', for decline is not limited to islands, but despite the oversimplification it is true that Bute's difficulties have been accentuated through insularity. Mr MacDonald also considers 'that local agencies on the Island of Bute be they local authorities or private enterprise no longer have the necessary funds to change the destiny of the island'. He believes it 'essential in order that a further decline in population be avoided that outside agencies be persuaded to act in the necessary fashion', the outside agencies being the central and regional governments.

Among the schemes suggested for public development are some advocated by earlier official reports, notably the expansion of tourism to an all-the-year-round activity, the development of suitable overspill industry, and the founding of an agricultural or technical college. This last suggestion might provide an alternative to a proposal for the establishment of a university on the island, which, although given serious consideration and examined by Professor Kenneth Alexander of Strathclyde University, may have been over-ambitious. Professor Alexander has been prominent also in helping to prepare and present evidence to support the claims for the building of a road bridge.

An interesting series of proposals concerning Bute are included in the 1970 *Firth of Clyde Study* by Professor Travis, which was published by the Scottish Tourist Board. A central idea was to make the island a national park, with agriculture and fishing continuing in their present roles, and the coast included in the Clyde National Waterpark. Areas of recreation would be carefully selected and sited, north Bute's wild moorland preserved, and the southern end protected by conservation. Ideas for improving Rothesay as a resort were also included.

It is worth pointing out that Bute folk are not standing still waiting for outside schemes to rescue their economy or restore their attractive holiday image. The redevelopment of Rothesay is already under way, with the reshaping of Ladeside and the town centre in progress. The large Ardencraig private house-building enterprise is well advanced, and the promotion of Rothesay as a conference centre, using assets like the Pavilion, which can cater for 1,200 delegates, and the splendidly equipped Glenburn Hotel, is attracting interest.

Delays in decision-making are often the result of a real dilemma rather than procrastination. The whole Clyde area is in a state of flux, and decisions made now may have far-reaching effect on an area of outstanding natural beauty. Bute like its neighbours lives under the threatening shadow of changes that could destroy the unique quality of its surroundings.

It should be pointed out also that, without underestimating the vital importance of tourism, there is another way of life for many in Bute. The successful and reasonably prosperous pattern of modern farming is worth safeguarding, and there is at least the nucleus of new economic development. One of the factors in the island's decline was the lack of new industries to replace the old ones, and in planning Bute's future role consideration must be given to setting up industries appropriate to the environment. Enterprises like the Bute Looms and Sea-food Industries are obviously on the right lines, but there is scope for greater development.

The inevitability of change is a fact of life that has to be faced—if not always accepted gladly. Bute, like other places of the Clyde, witnesses the passing of an age with mixed feelings. Progress is welcomed, but nostalgia remains for the things that are no more—the lost saints or the lost steamers, the independent worker or the self-employed fisherman, the memories of springs that will not return, or the dreams of summers that never were. But the sadness for the passing of the individual craftsman may be alleviated by the excitement of new crafts arising on the island, and the gloom caused by the loss of the old ships can be tempered by the sight of new vessels on the waters. Car-ferry services show steadily increasing returns, and an impressive new pier terminal was built in 1969. In 1972, for the first time in many years, there was the promise of an expanded timetable of sailings, the *Travis Report* recommended recreational planning for the area, and ambitious new projects were contemplated. The places of the Clyde are adapting themselves to a new age, and Bute is ready to take stock of its advantages as a holiday island, without surrendering completely its own way of life.

The latter reservation may appear to be something of a luxury in this day and age, but how could an island with such a long, continuous, and unbroken history of human activity forget its heritage? An island community should have an individuality which defines and identifies, but idealism must be tempered by realism. The twin truths remain that man cannot live by bread alone—but that bread is necessary to life. Since there is no virtue in a dying island or a decaying community, reality must be faced—but reality is built not only on facts, but on legend, which also plays a part in survival. As poetry so often outlasts statistics, so the place that cherishes and nurtures its legend can outlive a more prosaic neighbour. The modern dilemma of an island is how to preserve the legend without endangering the means of livelihood, how to arrest decline without sacrificing character.

In position and circumstance Bute has many unique features that complicate the finding of a solution. If decline is not to become synonomous with decay, the legend of the past must be combined with a vision for the future. The island must not only be a good place for people to live in, but also a place which can offer them a good living. Obviously tourism must be an important factor—but there are others. The island that over the centuries sheltered saints and resisted tyrants should be able to find the means in modern times of welcoming its visitors without surrendering its character, of retaining a satisfying and independent life of its own, while offering relaxation to holiday-makers who come to its shores.

THE ISLAND OF BUTE

This poem by Robin Munro appeared in the *Glasgow Herald*.

THE CLYDE COAST

I'm watching
my childhood
become a development
dreaming of ships in a field, lost like seagulls.

There are roads
on the sea
to take from the tide
all the power of our world,

and Cumbrae,
an embryo,
rests in a nuclear womb.
Dunoon sinks in holy protection.

Hamburg and
Rotterdam used
to be green, some one said,
but it's long since the avocets left.

My children
will learn how
the Metraport city was several places,
once touching a blue world we sailed on.

The poem crystallises the dream and the nightmare of those who know intimately and magically the blue world of Clyde waters, and who cherish the memory of a rare beauty while fearing the passing of something irreplaceable. The unique character and appeal of this Firth and the islands that lie at its heart may belong to the world of legend rather than fact— but that legend is the core of understanding, and the places of the Clyde carry their own secrets and their own mysteries within their names.

The waters of the Firth of Clyde have many shores to reach with each incoming tide. From Ailsa Craig, that craggy granite gannet-haunted rock, they run by way of Great and Little

Cumbraes, Kilbrannan and Inchmarnock, through sheltering Kyles and sheltered bays of Bute, past Toward and the Cloch to touch the curly Tail of Bank; and reach the muddy stretch to Broomielaw itself, or turn aside on pilgrimage to Holy Loch, Loch Goil, and on along the long way up Loch Long to come within a mile of turning Lomond salt.

Ships and men as well as tides have left their mark along these shores—it is 6,000 years since the first men came, seaborne upon the friendly Firth when forest, marsh, and mountain was all the land could offer. In the Bronze and Iron Ages they sailed towards Kintyre's blue-shadowed Mull on their way to build their cairns at Michael's point, or forts at Dunagoil. Then saintly ones in frailer crafts—Ninian, Marnoc, Blane, and Colmac—left their names around the holy isle of Bute, until less welcome tides brought Vikings down from northern parts.

The nearer years have seen the passage of all kinds of ships, or sorts of men. The Clyde has let them all come by, the saints and sinners, dukes and tinkers, kings and tattie-howkers, fools and oracles. In grey of winter mist or heather-tinted summer haze they came, the ships of peace and men of war, the fishing boats and pleasure steamers, the puffers and the coracles. All would know that distant view of Antrim's coast, the softly rounded Paps of Jura, and Arran's isle so deep asleep in peace beneath the Sleeping Warrior.

On the Isle of Bute each found some place to rest and live—on Glenvoidean and Kilmichael's gentle slopes, the crags of Dunagoil, the strands of St Ninian's and Inchmarnock, or the green vale of St Blane's. While up above was a world of moor and bracken, sky and curlew's calling, yet bounded ever by the Firth below. It scarcely needs the scratchings on the weathered stones or relics from the crumbling cairns to bring to mind the ends of older voyagers, whose days were lived as far far back as human mind can reach.

Many waters, many tides, move across the oceans of the world, but the tides and waters of this Firth move closest to

213

the men of Clyde who know them as their source. The tides that touch the shores of Corrie, Kames, and Cowal, the waves that break against the rocks of Garroch Head, the currents circling round Skipness, Inchmarnock, Cumbrae, Loch Ridden and Loch Striven, meet at last in Rothesay Bay, where ships found sheltered haven by the shores of Bute, and men of all times found an island they could call a home—an island of incredible richness in nature's gifts and works of men, an island cherished by its people and admired by its visitors, an island of quiet hills and lochs and bays, serene against the backdrop of the Sleeping Warrior—the Island of Bute.

BIBLIOGRAPHY

ATKINSON, R. J. C. *The Prehistoric People of Scotland*
BLAIN, JOHN. *History of Bute* (1880)
BLAIR, HUNTER. *John Patrick, 3rd Marquess of Bute* (1921)
——. *A Last Medley of Memoirs*
BLAKE, GEORGE. *The Firth of Clyde* (1952)
BOYCE, J. *The Geology of Arran and the Other Clyde Islands* (1872)
BROWN, A. *Kilchattan Past and Present* (1922)
BROWN, ALFRED. *Mollusca of the Firth of Clyde* (1878)
BROWN, IVOR. *Summer in Scotland* (1952)
CAMPBELL, MARION. *Birds of Mid-Argyll*
COCKER, W. D. *The Firth of Clyde*
COTON, R. H. *Decline of the Paddle Steamer* (1971)
DARLING, FRASER. *Natural History in the Highlands and Islands* (1947)
DENT, ALAN. *Preludes and Studies*
DOWNIE, R. ANGUS. *Bute and the Cumbraes* (1934)
DUCKWORTH and LANGMUIR. *Clyde River and Other Steamers*
DUNCAN, JAMES. *Craftsmen of Bute* (1953)
EYRE TODD, GEORGE. *Famous Scottish Burghs* (1923)
FERRIER, JOHN. *Robert Thom's Water Cuts*
GIBSON, J. A. *Mammals of Bute* (1970)
GRANT. *History of Burgh Schools in Scotland*
HAMILTON. *The Industrial Revolution in Scotland* (1932)
HEWISON, J. KING. *The Isle of Bute in the Olden Times*, 1 (1893)
——. *The Isle of Bute in the Olden Times*, 2 (1895)
HONEYMAN, T. J. *Introducing Leslie Hunter* (1937)
HOUSE, JACK. *Down the Clyde* (1959)
HUNTER and MUNRO. *The Clyde* (1907)
JOHNSTON, W. J. *History of Celtic Place Names of Scotland*
JONES. *History of the Vikings* (1968)
KAY, JAMES. *The Rocks of Bute* (1909)
LAWSON. *Glimpses of Rothesay 50 Years Ago* (1923)
LEACH, ALLAN. *Rothesay Tramways 1882–1936* (1969)

LINDSAY, MAURICE. *The Lowlands of Scotland*
MACBRIDE, MACKENZIE. *Firth of Clyde* (1911)
MACCALLIEN, W. J. *The Rocks of Bute* (1909)
MACCULLOCH, J. *The Geology of the Western Isles of Scotland* (1819)
MACDONALD, MALCOLM. *The Island of Bute/A Study in Decline* (1971)
MACFIE. *Bute Record of Rural Affairs* (1860)
MACKENZIE, JOHN. *Country Editor* (1968)
MACLAGAN, F. A. *The Flora of Bute* (1939)
MACQUEEN, ANDREW. *Echoes of the Old Clyde Paddle-Wheels* (1924)
MCWILLIAM, J. M. *The Birds of the Island of Bute* (1927)
——. *Birds of the Firth of Clyde* (1936)
MARSHALL, DOROTHY. *History of Bute* (1970)
MARTIN, M. *Description of the Western Isles* (1716)
MAXWELL, DONALD. *The Book of the Clyde*
MILLAR, W. J. *The Clyde* (1888)
MUNRO, NEIL. *Para Handy* (1931)
O'DELL, A. C. and WALTON, K. *The Highlands and Islands of Scotland* (1962)
PATERSON, ALAN. *The Golden Years of the Clyde Steamers* (1969)
PIGGOTT, STUART. *The Prehistoric Peoples of Scotland* (1962)
PLAYFAIR, GILES. *Kean*
POWELL. *The Celts*
RAITT and PRYDE. *Scotland* (1934)
REID, J. E. *History of the County of Bute* (1864)
REID, J. M. *Scotland Past and Present* (1959)
SIMPSON, W. DOUGLAS. *Rothesay Castle* (1952)
SOMERVILLE, CAMERON. *Colour on the Clyde* (1961)
THOMAS, JOHN. *North British Railway*, vol 1 (1969)
WATSON, W. J. *History of Celtic Place Names of Scotland* (1926)
WILLIAMSON, JAMES. *The Clyde Passenger Steamers* (1904)

Bute Record of Rural Affairs (1839)
Calendar of Documents Relating to Scotland (1307–1509)
Calendar of State Papers (1858)
Clyde Programme (1898)
Fowler's Commercial Directory of Scotland (1834)
History of Rothesay Public School (1955)
New Statistical Account of Scotland (1845)

BIBLIOGRAPHY

A Pageant of the Brandanes (1951)
Statistical Account of Scotland (1791)
A Study of Tourism in the Clyde Area (1968)
Third Statistical Account of Scotland (1962)
Transactions of the Buteshire Natural History Society (1907–71)

ACKNOWLEDGEMENTS

The author gratefully acknowledges his indebtedness to those who have helped in the making of *The Island of Bute*, especially to Mary Munro for research and work on the book, and original material on Edmund Kean.

Others who provided material and photographs, and gave freely of their knowledge, experience and time included Miss Catherine Armet, Mr Daniel Boag, Mr Robert Crozier, Mr J. A. Duguid, Dr John Ferrier, Mr Andrew Knox, Mr Allan Leach, Miss Catherine McFarlane, Mr John MacKenzie, Mr Ian Maclagan, Mr and Mrs J. Maclagan, Miss Dorothy N. Marshall, Mr Roderick Middleton, Mr R. A. Milligan, Mr Robin Munro, Mr Douglas Nicholson, Mr M. O'Dowd, Mr D. Ritchie, and Mrs G. T. S. Stevens.

The poem *Clyde Coast* first appeared in the *Glasgow Herald*.

INDEX

Italic numerals indicate illustration pages

INDEX

INDEX

222

INDEX